Celebrate His Love

DR. DAVID JEREMIAH

with Dr. David Jeremiah

Published by Walk Thru the Bible Ministries, Atlanta, Georgia.

Unless otherwise indicated, Scripture verses quoted are taken from the NEW KING JAMES VERSION.

Printed in the United States of America.

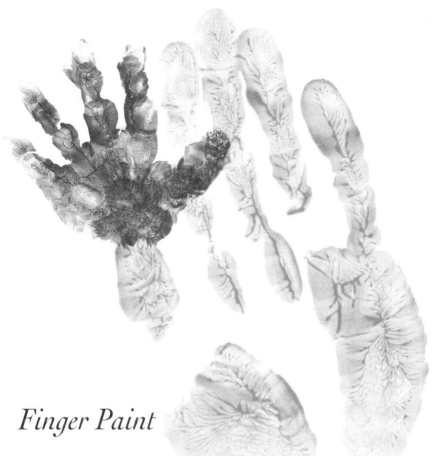

Finger Paint

Holding the hand of my grandson creates a sense of joy and awe that is beyond description. His little hand gets lost in mine and he doesn't want to be held too tightly to restrict his activity. Holding that little hand turns my mind and heart to an awareness of the love of God that brings new joy to me especially at this season when we celebrate the birth of God's Son, Jesus.

When Jesus was born, God touched earth with the strength and power of the Creator of the universe. With the same grace that formed the first man and woman, he fashioned a tiny hand that would one day be nailed to a cross for you and me.

The greatest gift you can give this holiday season is the touch of your hand on the life of someone who does not know Christ as Savior.

Introduce someone to the Christchild and let them know He grew, became a man, and gave His life for them. Your joy will be shared by the angels when someone accepts His gift of eternal life.

Contents

Dr. David Jeremiah and Turning Point

D r. David Jeremiah is the founder of Turning Point, a ministry committed to providing Christians with sound Bible teaching relevant to today's changing times through radio broadcasts, audiocassette series, and books. Dr. Jeremiah's "common sense" teaching on topics such as family, stress, the New Age, angels, and biblical prophecy forms the foundation of Turning Point.

Dr. Jeremiah is the senior pastor of Shadow Mountain Community Church in El Cajon near San Diego, California, where he also serves as Chancellor of Christian Heritage College. He and his wife, Donna, have four children.

In 1982, Dr. Jeremiah brought the same solid teaching to San Diego television that he shares weekly with his congregation. Shortly thereafter, Turning Point expanded its ministry to radio. Dr. Jeremiah's inspiring messages are currently broadcast weekly from more than 900 radio outlets.

Because Dr. Jeremiah desires to know his listening audience, he travels nationwide holding Spiritual Enrichment conferences that touch the hearts and lives of many. According to Dr. Jeremiah, "At some point in time, everyone reaches a turning point, and for every person that moment is unique, an experience to hold onto forever. There's so much changing in today's world that sometimes it's difficult to choose the right path. Turning Point offers people an understanding of God's Word, as well as the opportunity to make a difference in their lives."

Dr. Jeremiah has authored numerous books including *Escape the Coming Night* (Revelation), *The Handwriting on the Wall* (Daniel), *Turning Toward Joy* (Philippians), *Turning Toward Integrity* (James), *Invasion of Other Gods* (New Age), *Overcoming Loneliness*, *What the Bible Says About Angels*, *The Power of Encouragement*, *Prayer—The Great Adventure*, *God in You* (Holy Spirit), *Gifts from God* (Parenting), and *Jesus' Final Warning*.

About This Study Guide

The purpose of this Turning Point study guide is to reinforce Dr. David Jeremiah's dynamic, in-depth teaching on Christmas and aid the reader in applying biblical truth to his or her daily life. This study guide is designed to be used in conjunction with Dr. Jeremiah's *Celebrate His Love* audiocassette series, but it may also be used by itself for personal or group Bible study.

Structure of the Lessons

Each lesson is based on one of the tapes in the *Celebrate His Love* audiocassette series and focuses on a specific subject in Scripture. Each lesson is composed of the following elements:

✒ Outline

The outline at the beginning of the lesson gives a clear, concise picture of the subject being studied and provides a helpful framework for readers as they listen to Dr. Jeremiah's teaching.

✒ Overview

The overview summarizes Dr. Jeremiah's teaching on the subject being studied in the lesson. Readers should refer to the biblical references in their own Bibles as they study the overview.

✒ Application

This section contains a variety of questions designed to help readers dig deeper into the lesson and the Scriptures, and to apply the lesson to their daily lives. For Bible study groups or Sunday school classes, these questions will provide a springboard for group discussion and interaction.

✒ Did You Know?

This section presents an interesting fact, historical note, or insight which adds a point of interest to the preceding lesson.

Using This Guide for Group Study

The lessons in this study guide are suitable for Sunday school classes, small-group studies, elective Bible studies, or home Bible study groups. Each person in the group should have his or her own study guide.

When possible, the study guide should be used with the corresponding tape series. You may wish to assign the study guide as homework prior to the group meeting and then use the meeting time to listen to the tape and discuss the lesson.

For Continuing Study

A complete catalog of Dr. Jeremiah's materials for personal and group study is available through Turning Point. To obtain a catalog, additional study guides, or more information about Turning Point, call 1-800-947-1993 or write to: Turning Point, P.O. Box 3838, San Diego, CA 92163.

Dr. Jeremiah's "Turning Point" radio broadcast is currently heard on more than 900 radio outlets. Contact your local Christian radio station or Turning Point for program times in your area.

Celebrate His Love

INTRODUCTION

Sitting in my air-conditioned office in Southern California watching the delivery man jump from his truck in short pants, arms loaded with Christmas deliveries, presents a very different image from the Currier and Ives white country church spires against a backdrop of juniper and pines dusted with snow.

The scenes of Christmas are varied and unique to geography and family traditions. In days gone by, the church was the center of community activity and signaled the beginning of Christmas celebrations. Now the retail stores begin to display Christmas decorations in early fall and colorful catalogs arrive in the mail in September. Strategically timed television commercials tease the children with the latest toy craze. News people report on the toy in short supply and seem to take pride in reporting the "run" on the toy stores.

That indescribable longing for a picture-perfect holiday eludes most of us, and yet something keeps the commercial side of Christmas growing yearly.

The joy and hope of the Christmas season can be confused and crowded out if we do not purpose in our hearts and minds to celebrate and proclaim the true message of the season.

In this study, I will examine some of the seldom-studied facets of Christmas, from the silence and solitude of that "silent night," to the status of the shepherds in the fields, to the common humanity of the Baby so inconspicuously born in a dirty stable somewhere in Bethlehem. The point of these incisive studies is not only to observe Christmas, but to understand it as God would have us understand it; to experience it as nearly as we can 2,000 years after the fact; and to let it touch and change our lives as Jesus Christ Himself wants it to.

This study opens with a topic that draws together the various dimensions of the Christmas season: the music we hear just about everywhere we go. Could it be we've become so accustomed to it we not only neglect to hear the words, but we don't even question why this is a season of song and music to begin with?

From the melodies and harmonies of songs in our culture as well as in Scripture, we will examine the silence of that silent night; the wonder of an event that took place in a corner of Jerusalem's least significant suburb; the miracle of God incarnated as a human baby; the significance of His title at birth; His name and its impact; how to love Jesus at Christmas-time; His identity as a "common" human being; our call to remember Him; and a stimulating challenge to make the Word of God our top priority for the dawning New Year.

It's a journey that will be most beneficial if you make it with your Bible readily at hand, with the first two chapters of Luke clearly bookmarked. If you can obtain one, an old church hymnal (containing traditional Christmas hymns) or Christmas songbook may be helpful as well.

I am not suggesting you eliminate the time-honored traditions of the season and to help you incorporate some of our family activities we have scattered throughout this study guide holiday ideas to help you create celebrations that are meaningful.

Most important—keep readily at hand all the memories, questions, wonder, nostalgia, and emotional trappings of Christmas past. They're sure to play a part in your study of God's Word this holiday season.

CELEBRATE His Love
David Jeremiah

The Joy and Music of Christmas

In this lesson we examine the universal phenomenon of the music of joy and celebration at Christmas.

OUTLINE

One of the hallmarks of the Christmas season around the world is the playing and singing of holiday hymns and music. In light of that, have we ever stopped to ask ourselves why this is so? And even more important, where did this music of joy and celebration originate?

The answers to these questions—taken directly from the pages of Scripture—are sure to deepen their meaning.

I. There Is Joy and Music at Christmas Because Old Testament Prophecies Were Fulfilled

II. There Is Joy and Music at Christmas Because the Problem of Sin Has Been Resolved

III. There Is Joy and Music at Christmas Because the Pain of the Lowly and Forgotten Has Been Remembered

IV. There Is Joy and Music at Christmas Because the Possibility of Peace Is Renewed in Our Hearts

V. There Is Joy and Music at Christmas Because the Purpose of Life Is Illustrated in the Songs of the Nativity

VI. There Is Joy and Music at Christmas Because the Predictions of Christ's Second Coming Are Secure

OVERVIEW

Christianity is a religion of song. Agnosticism has no carols. Confucianism and Brahminism have no anthems or alleluias. Dreary, weird dirges reveal no hope for the present or for the future. Christianity, however, is filled with music. Only the message of Christ puts a song in a person's heart.

When you have Christ in your heart, when you know what Christmas is all about, something changes inside of you, and a melody starts to form that you can't really control. It is unlike any other belief system.

As we read the stories of Christmas in the book of Luke, we find six different songs recorded almost back-to-back: the "Beatitude of Elizabeth," when she was visited by Mary; the "Magnificat of Mary," Mary's song; the "Benedictus of Zacharias," the father of John the Baptist; the "Song of Simeon," when he was presented with the Christ Child at the temple; the "Evangel Song" of the angel of the Lord over the plains; and, finally, the "Gloria" of the angelic hosts. When Jesus came into the world, poetry expressed itself and music was reborn.

Why do we sing during the Christmas season? Everywhere we go, every time we turn on the radio or television, every time we go to a shopping center, someone is playing or singing Christmas music. If we didn't know what it was all about, it could really be irritating! There's nothing worse than knowing that somebody is truly filled with joy, but not understanding why—wishing you had it, but not understanding how to get it.

Why are we so filled with joy and music at this season of the year? What is it about Christmas that makes us want to sing?

Several reasons are illustrated by the songs in Luke 2.

There Is Joy and Music at Christmas Because Old Testament Prophecies Were Fulfilled

When Christ was born, one of the reasons for great songs in the hearts of people was that the prophecies of the Old Testament had at last been fulfilled.

In Simeon's song recorded in Luke chapter 2:25-32, we get some understanding of the Jews' longing for the fulfillment of prophecy. "And behold, there was a man in Jerusalem whose name was

Simeon, and this man was just and devout, waiting for the Consolation of Israel, and the Holy Spirit was upon him. And it had been revealed to him by the Holy Spirit that he would not see death before he had seen the Lord's Christ."

Somehow, for some reason, Simeon had been given a word from the Lord that he would live until the Messiah was born. Every day he probably wondered, "Is this the day when prophecy will be fulfilled?" All of his life he had longed for the Messiah. Simeon was well-acquainted with Isaiah 40-55, which tells about the nature of the coming of the Messiah. The joy of seeing those prophecies fulfilled kept Simeon alive until at last, one day, in the temple, he had the joy of seeing the Messiah Himself. Simeon, then, is an illustration of all those who awaited the coming of Christ.

The Old Testament is filled with prophecies of the coming of Messiah in such a specific way that most Jewish people had a tendency to read right over it and miss the significance of what the prophets were saying. Micah, for instance, said that Messiah would be born in Bethlehem. Daniel actually gave a timetable of how this was going to happen. Isaiah said that Messiah would be born of a virgin, something that had never happened before. Jeremiah said Christ's birth would be accompanied by the slaughter of many children. Hosea revealed that at a certain time they would have to go into Egypt to spare the life of the Child.

All of these prophecies were given 500 to 700 years before the birth of Christ; and there were devout Jews who every day would read the Scriptures, ponder these verses, and wonder, "Will that happen in my lifetime? Will I see the Messiah?"

So, when Christ was born, and it became apparent that this was indeed the Messiah, they were filled with joy, and they burst forth into song and excitement.

Consider the incredible nature of the prophecies concerning the coming of Christ. For example, in 700 B.C. Micah prophesied that Messiah would be born in Bethlehem. What possibility is there of any man, by his own wisdom, predicting the birthplace of someone not yet born? There is no possibility at all. If we examine every piece of American literature down to the year 1830, we will not find one phrase even suggesting that a future president of the United States would some day be born in Harlan County, Kentucky. But Micah the prophet put his finger on one of the smallest countries in the world,

Israel, designated one of the twelve provinces in which the Messiah was to be born—namely, Judah—and within that province, put his finger on one small village called Bethlehem, and said it was there that Messiah would be born. David is the only king of Judah who had ever been born in Bethlehem. All the other kings, generation after generation until Judah fell, were born in the royal city of Jerusalem. Most of them probably were born in the palace. So, if prophets of Micah's day had guessed the birthplace of Jesus, they never would have guessed Bethlehem. They would have guessed Jerusalem, where kings would normally be born.

It was only due to a Roman edict concerning taxation that Joseph and Mary were in Bethlehem when Jesus was born. It was a pagan edict that sent them to the very place where Micah said Jesus would be born.

When Christ was born and it became apparent to the few who gathered around the scene that this was indeed the Messiah, we can understand why they were filled with joy and became so excited they couldn't do anything but burst into song.

We sing at Christmastime because the prophecies of the Old Testament were fulfilled, and we are reminded of that truth.

THERE IS JOY AND MUSIC AT CHRISTMAS BECAUSE THE PROBLEM OF SIN HAS BEEN RESOLVED

Once and for all, the sin problem has been solved. If we look back to Bethlehem and back to the birth of Jesus, we have to look back through the empty tomb. We have to look back through the Cross. We have to look back through the Garden of Gethsemane. And as we look back, we come to the manger, and we know that Bethlehem was the answer to the question that plagued every heart: How can a man know God?

In the Old Testament, in faith believers brought sacrifices in order to know God in the Old Testament way. But there also was the promise of the Lamb of God who would come and be slain for everyone, thus sin could forever be put to rest for those who would trust in the Messiah.

I think that's what Zacharias was talking about in Luke 1:68-79:

> Blessed is the Lord God of Israel, for He has visited
> and redeemed His people, and has raised up a horn of

salvation for us . . . that we should be saved from our
enemies . . . , to perform the mercy promised to our
fathers and to remember His holy covenant . . . , to
grant us that we, being delivered from the hand of
our enemies . . . , to give knowledge of salvation to
His people by the remission of their sins, through the
tender mercy of our God . . .

Zacharias understood that the coming of Jesus Christ was for a
specific purpose, that He might ultimately be the Redeemer.

Why is there joy and singing at Christmas? For the same reason
that there is joy and singing in heaven when one sinner repents. When
salvation becomes a reality, when we understand what it truly means
to be forgiven, to have the burden of sin lifted off us, to know that we
never have to stand in judgment for our sin, that is a reason for song.

THERE IS JOY AND MUSIC AT CHRISTMAS BECAUSE THE PAIN
OF THE LOWLY AND FORGOTTEN HAS BEEN REMEMBERED

Listen to Mary's song, beginning in Luke 1:46:

'My soul magnifies the Lord, and my spirit has
rejoiced in God my Savior. For He has regarded the
lowly state of His maidservant; for behold, henceforth
all generations will call me blessed. For He who is
mighty has done great things for me, and holy is His
name. And His mercy is on those who fear Him from
generation to generation. He has shown strength with
His arm; He has scattered the proud in the imagina-
tion of their hearts. He has put down the mighty from
their thrones, and exalted the lowly. He has filled the
hungry with good things, and the rich He has sent
away empty. He has helped His servant Israel . . .'

Every Christmas, God is saying to the downtrodden, the
oppressed, and the exploited of mankind, "Be of good cheer. I am
your friend, and I am your champion. I have sent My Son with good
news for the poor, to proclaim and release captives, and to set at
liberty those who are oppressed."

Why is there joy at Christmas? Because no matter who we are, no matter how poor we are, no matter how unimportant we may feel, every Christmas there is a renewal within us of this message: Christ has chosen to be among the common people. He came in a common way, not born in a palace but in a manger, not surrounded by kings but by shepherds, to make sure that none of us, no matter who we are, no matter how insignificant we may think ourselves to be, none of us are out of the sphere of the love of God at Christmas.

THERE IS JOY AND MUSIC AT CHRISTMAS BECAUSE THE POSSIBILITY OF PEACE IS RENEWED IN OUR HEARTS

In more than a few past wars, the warring nations would call a cease-fire for Christmas Day. They would agree that on Christmas Day they wouldn't shoot at each other, drop bombs on each other, or try to destroy one another. Then, of course, the day after Christmas they would start killing each other again.

As strange as that custom has been, in a wonderful way it is a mute testimony to the purpose for which Christ came—to bring peace. Wasn't that the message that the angels proclaimed in Luke 2:8-14?

> Now there were in the same country shepherds living out in the fields, keeping watch over their flock by night. And behold, an angel of the Lord stood before them, and the glory of the Lord shone around them, and they were greatly afraid. Then the angel said to them, "Do not be afraid, for behold, I bring you good tidings of great joy which will be to all people. For there is born to you this day in the city of David a Savior, who is Christ the Lord. And this will be the sign to you: You will find a Babe wrapped in swaddling cloths, lying in a manger." And suddenly there was with the angel a multitude of the heavenly host praising God and saying: "Glory to God in the highest, and on earth peace, goodwill toward men!"

We sing at Christmas because within our hearts there is hope of peace. Today, there are many places in our world where peace is not

Celebrate His Love

a word in anyone's vocabulary. Yet every Christian knows that there is coming a time when peace will reign on this earth. Each Christmas season, a kind of new hope is born in our hearts—that though the outlook may be dark, and the only darkness we may see is out there, we may not feel it here. The Prince of Peace has come, and with Him the faith that someday men will beat their swords into plowshares and their spears into pruning hooks and we shall be at peace.

THERE IS JOY AND MUSIC AT CHRISTMAS BECAUSE THE PURPOSE OF LIFE IS ILLUSTRATED IN THE SONGS OF THE NATIVITY

Throughout all of the songs we find this note of glory and praise to the Father. Mary's song begins, "My soul magnifies the Lord, and my spirit has rejoiced in God my Savior."

Elizabeth was so full of joy and praise for her God that when she met Mary, the baby jumped in her womb for the joy of being in the presence of the Messiah.

Zacharias, in his "Benedictus," said, "Blessed is the Lord God of Israel."

And the message of the angels was "Glory to God in the highest!"

What is the real purpose of life for all of us? According to the Westminster Catechism, it is to glorify God and to enjoy Him forever. And in the message of Christmas we find that wonderful story. Everywhere we read the songs of Christmas in the Book of Luke, they are extolling the glory of God, praising God, and blessing God.

THERE IS JOY AND MUSIC AT CHRISTMAS BECAUSE PREDICTIONS OF CHRIST'S SECOND COMING ARE SECURE

As we read the prophecies of Micah, Jeremiah, Hosea, Daniel, and Isaiah, and we follow them through 600 or 700 years, all the way up to when Jesus was born in Bethlehem, we are amazed at the accuracy of prophecies that could reveal exactly where Messiah would be born. Or that Isaiah could say, "Born of a virgin." Or that Jeremiah could foretell a slaughter of children connected with that birth. Or that Hosea could reveal a flight into Egypt to avoid danger. Yet all of those same prophets have told us that Messiah who came the first time is coming again.

How accurately will those prophecies be fulfilled? Just as accurately as the first prophecies were fulfilled. Many things mentioned in the songs of Luke weren't fulfilled at Bethlehem—because they are yet to be fulfilled when Christ comes again.

Why is there joy at Christmas? Because the same Jesus who came the first time is coming again.

APPLICATION

1. Make a list of all the Bible-based Christmas hymns you can think of, then answer the following:

   a. Which songs mention the Divine nature of Jesus Christ at His birth?

   Which specific phrases?

   b. Which songs refer to the fulfillment of prophecy at His birth?

   Which specific phrases?

c. Which songs refer to His eventual reign as King and Messiah on earth?

Which specific phrases?

d. Which songs refer to His love and care for all mankind?

Which specific phrases?

e. Which songs refer to the songs found in the Bible?

Which specific phrases?

2. In Mary's song (Luke 1:46-55):

   a. What is Mary's emotional response to the message she is given?

   b. Upon whom is her focus?

   How do you know?

   c. What future personal circumstances does she not mention?

   d. What is the significance of her statement in verse 55?

Celebrate His Love

3. In the song of Zacharias (Luke 1:68-79):

    a. How many future deeds or activities of the Messiah does he mention?

    b. What are those, in which verses?

    c. Why is God doing these things, according to the words of Zacharias (vv. 72-73)?

    d. What office will his son (John the Baptizer) fill, according to vv. 76-77?

e. How does this relate to the last Old Testament book (see Malachi 3:1; 4:5-6)?

4. In the song of the angelic host (Luke 2:14):

   a. Who ultimately is glorified by the birth of Messiah?

   b. What do you think the phrase "on earth peace" refers to specifically?

   c. To what does "goodwill toward men" refer?

Whose goodwill?

Displayed how?

5. Which of the events or circumstances displayed in these three songs do you think have already taken place?

6. Which events or circumstances do you think are yet to occur?

7. If biblical "hope" is the present assurance of a future certainty, how would you describe the "hope" of the Christmas season?

DID YOU KNOW?

Some of the traditional Christmas hymns are tremendous repositories of Christian theology. For example, if one reads all the verses of Wesley's "Hark! The Herald Angels Sing," there can be found such doctrines as the virgin birth, the deity of Christ, the incarnation, the depravity of mankind, the *kenosis* (humbling) of Christ, His sinlessness, and His Second Coming, to name a few. Perhaps the next time we celebrate Christmas, it would serve us well to acquire and read all the words to some of the historical hymns of the season.

Celebrate His Love

Gingerbread Cookie Ornaments

1/2 cup dark brown sugar
1 cup butter
2 teas. baking soda
1 teas. salt
4 tbls. sugar
1 cup molasses
1 teas. cinnamon
1/2 teas. ginger
1/4 teas. nutmeg
1/4 teas. cloves
3 cups flour

Cream together butter and sugars. Add molasses and blend well. Add remaining ingredients to mixture and stir well. (If dough is too soft, add a little flour; if too crumbly, add a few drops of milk or water.)

Divide dough into fourths and wrap each section in plastic wrap. Refrigerate at least two hours.

On a well-floured surface, roll out dough, one fourth at a time, to 1/4 inch thickness. Cut with flour-dusted cookie cutters and place on ungreased cookie sheet. Punch a hole for hanging on top of each cookie with a drinking straw or wooden skewer.

Bake at 350 degrees for 8 to 10 minutes or until set.

Cool completely on wire rack, then decorate the cookies using icing, candies, and colored sugars. Let the children express their creativity.

It is fun to make a custom cookie ornament by writing a name in icing and tying it to a package for a teacher or special friend. Remember: Don't worry about making mistakes; you can eat them!

The Silence
of Christmas

*In this lesson we contemplate the significance of the
isolation, humility, and solitary silence of the Messiah's birth.*

OUTLINE

In our world today there is never a time of total silence. Never does
the world come to a complete stop—with one exception: Christmas
Day. Nobody goes anywhere on Christmas Day. Everybody stays at
home. Nobody is on the highways. Nobody is out and about. The
whole day is a quiet day, unlike any other day we celebrate throughout the year.

    I. A Silent Night at the Inn of Bethlehem

   II. A Silent Night on the Hillsides Outside of Bethlehem

Frederick Buechner has written a book entitled *A Room Called Remember*. In this book he tells the story of a snowstorm that took place in New York City in 1947. He said it was an incredible thing. Flakes just kept coming down, and before long, all of the streets were covered. There was no wind, so the snow didn't blow. It just stayed. Pretty soon, all the traffic in the city was stopped. The subways shut down. Nobody could go anywhere. Everything came to a complete, total stop. Buechner said the thing that overwhelmed him was the silence of it all. He said there was nothing going on in the city. When people stopped to listen to the noise of the city to which they had become so accustomed, there wasn't any. It was total silence.

A Silent Night at the Inn of Bethlehem

That must have been the way it was on the first Christmas. Luke 2:1-7 tells us it happened like this:

> And it came to pass in those days that a decree went out from Caesar Augustus that all the world should be registered. This census first took place while Quirinius was governing Syria. So all went to be registered, everyone to his own city. Joseph also went up from Galilee, out of the city of Nazareth, into Judea, to the city of David, which is called Bethlehem, because he was of the house and lineage of David, to be registered with Mary, his betrothed wife, who was with child. So it was, that while they were there, the days were completed for her to be delivered. And she brought forth her firstborn Son, and wrapped Him in swaddling cloths, and laid Him in a manger, because there was no room for them in the inn.

This story—so familiar to us—is nevertheless amazing. Hundreds of years before this event, Micah the prophet told everybody it was going to happen. And not only did he reveal that it was going to happen, but he told where it was going to happen! Not only did he single out the town of Bethlehem, but because there were two Bethlehems, he told which of the two it would be. We read in Micah 5:2, "But you, Bethlehem Ephrathah, though you are little among the thousands of Judah, yet out of you shall come forth to Me the One to be Ruler in Israel, whose goings forth are from of old, from everlasting." It is incredible that this prophecy was fulfilled as it was in the Christmas story. Think for a moment how—if the Roman census edict had gone out in a different way at a different time, everything would have been changed.

If the conception of the Virgin Mary had taken place six months earlier, Jesus would have been born in Nazareth of Galilee and carried to Bethlehem in Mary's arms. If the conception had taken place six months later Mary would have already returned to Nazareth, and the Babe would have been born in Nazareth of Galilee. But the edict went out, the conception took place, at exactly the right moment Mary and Joseph were in Bethlehem Ephrathah, and in that moment of time—as Micah the Prophet foretold—Jesus Christ was born and became one of us.

I don't understand all of this, but Luke 2:7 tells us that Mary brought forth her own child. She delivered her own baby. Where were the midwives? Where was the innkeeper and his wife? Where was anyone to help? No one was there. Mary, alone in a quiet place, in a moment of silence, brought forth her child. And into that silent night burst a tiny baby's cry.

It was that cry that gave hope to a lost world. Someone had come to fix things. Many misunderstood it at the time. Many thought He was going to take away Roman bondage. Little did they know that He had in mind a bondage greater and more eternal than Roman bondage. When that little One cried, it meant that the Messiah had come to earth. In that quiet moment, God had become human, so that as the God-man He could wrap His arms around a lost humanity, and bring that lost humanity to the Father.

A Silent Night on the Hillsides Outside Bethlehem

On the hillside outside of Bethlehem, it was in the cooler season of the year. Shepherds were out in the fields keeping watch over their flocks by night. Nothing special was supposed to happen that night. It was like all the other winter nights when they cared for their sheep and watched over their flocks.

All of a sudden, in that quiet night on the hillside outside

Bethlehem there was an interruption. Just as the Baby had broken the silence at His birth, the heavenly choirs came to break the silence of that hillside. In Luke 2:8-14 we read:

> Now there were in the same country shepherds living out in the fields, keeping watch over their flock by night. And behold, an angel of the Lord stood before them, and the glory of the Lord shone around them, and they were greatly afraid. Then the angel said to them, "Do not be afraid, for behold, I bring you good tidings of great joy which will be to all people. For there is born to you this day in the city of David a Savior, who is Christ the Lord. And this will be the sign to you: You will find a Babe wrapped in swaddling cloths, lying in a manger." And suddenly there was with the angel a multitude of the heavenly host praising God and saying: "Glory to God in the highest, and on earth peace, good will toward men!"

If we had orchestrated this, if we had written the script, if we were the ones doing this pageant, would we have introduced the Lord Jesus Christ for the very first time to a group of shepherds? We've seen so many Christmas programs that most of us are conditioned to think, "Who else?" But in that day it would have been the last thought in your mind, because shepherds were considered ceremonially unclean. They were not allowed to worship in the temple. They were not allowed to go to court and bear witness, because they were the least of all. So God, who chose Bethlehem, the least of all the cities, also chose shepherds, who were the least of all men.

And in the quietness of a silent night, He broke in upon the countryside with an angelic host, praising God, and giving the first gospel message ever preached about the coming of Jesus Christ. What an incredible event!

What was that message? It was the message we need to listen to today: "Fear not." The circumstances into which Jesus was born are very much the circumstances in which we find our Christmas being celebrated today.

A lot of people "celebrate" Christmas with fear. Yet that first

Christmas message was, "Don't be afraid." The answer to our fears comes in the person of Jesus Christ.

The Word of God says the ultimate fear is our fear of death. What do we do with death? We need someone who has overcome it, and that's who Jesus was. He came to overcome death and take away fear.

The angels also proclaimed peace and good will toward men. In fact, in that first gospel message, the angels proclaimed to the shepherds every message we need for our lives today. But don't get caught up in the song, for the real message was in the Son. It was in the person of Jesus Christ himself.

It was a silent night near the inn at Bethlehem. A Baby cried, and nothing has been the same since. It was a silent night outside of Bethlehem where the shepherds watched their flocks, and the angels came and proclaimed the Gospel of Jesus Christ, and nothing has been the same since. And for many of us, it was a silent night, a quiet moment, when, in the deepest recesses of our hearts, we knew something was wrong, something was missing. Someone had told us that Jesus Christ came to fix all of that. And in that quiet moment, in that silent night, we invited the Savior of the world to be the Savior of our life. We accepted the one who came to be our Savior and Lord.

Many years ago, my wife and I visited Bethlehem, where there is a church called the Church of the Nativity. Though it is 100 feet by 70 feet in size, you can get into the church only one way. The door into the church is not much higher than a child, and it is only a couple of feet wide. To go into the church, people must—one at a time bend down, stoop, and walk through the door.

I remember thinking, "What an interesting reminder to all of us that entering the kingdom of God is not something that happens in a group. It is an individual experience. Knowing Jesus Christ is like getting into that church. You have to stoop down."

Too often, that's the last thing we are willing to do. We are too caught up in ourselves. We are going it alone, thinking we've got it all together.

Then, suddenly or gradually, the load of life's problems on our shoulders finally makes us stoop down. Sometimes it is a moment of reality when we realize that the Word of God says, "There is a way that seems right unto a man, but that way ends in death." The world would have us believe that we can come to Christ and embrace the Savior through our own efforts, but the Word of God says we must come to Him bowed down in humility, one at a time.

Would it not be a good thing for all of us in the midst of all the frenzied activity of Christmas, to get away for a short time and mediate on what this story really means and how it touches our lives?

Sometimes the most important voices we ever hear are the voices that interrupt the quietness. If you are not sure where you are with that One who came, you need to let Him speak to your heart.

APPLICATION

1. Read Luke 2:4.
   a. Why did Joseph and Mary have to be in Bethlehem?

   b. Why was that significant, in light of:

   Micah 5:2?

   2 Samuel 7:16-17?

2. If you were watching for Messiah at the time of His birth, what would you have expected?

How does that differ from what actually happened?

3. Read 1 Chronicles 11:2; 17:6; and Psalm 78:70-72.
   a. What groups of people were the "shepherds" of Israel in the Old Testament?

   b. What group of people would have been the designated "shepherds" of Israel at the time of Christ?

   c. To whom did that group of people probably expect God to announce the arrival of Messiah?

   d. To whom did the angels announce Messiah's arrival?

e. Why do you think He did it this way? (See Jeremiah 10:21; 23:1; 25:34.)

4. Read Ezekiel 34:2-16.
   a. What parallels can you see between the bad shepherds in Ezekiel and the religious leaders at the time of Christ's birth?

   b. What parallels can you see between God as the Shepherd of His people, and statements Christ made during His earthly ministry?

   c. What events spoken of in this passage apparently took place at the birth of Christ?

   d. What events spoken of in this passage have not yet taken place?

e. How might the angelic announcement to real shepherds have reminded Jews of this passage?

5. Read Psalm 78:49; 2 Kings 6:7; 19:35; Zechariah 10:3.
   a. Why might the shepherds have been frightened at the appearance of an angelic being (Luke 2:9)?

   b. What might they have been expecting to follow such an appearance?

   c. What, instead, is proclaimed to them?

   d. What, then, is the theme of the angelic proclamation in Luke 2:14?

e. What is the shepherds' response?

DID YOU KNOW?

Although most "nativity scenes" picture the Baby Jesus lying in a manger constructed of wood, nearly all mangers found in the archeological digs of Israel were quite different. Used for water or for fodder, they consisted of a rectangular trough carved out of a single piece of limestone or basalt—making them look something like a miniature stone tomb. What this means, of course, is that when at His birth Jesus was wrapped in swaddling cloths and laid in a manger, it was a picture of precisely what would be done with His body following His crucifixion.

Celebrate His Love

Light Up Your World

Watch for candles on sale tables throughout the year and gather an assortment of sizes and colors that fit your color scheme. All sizes and shapes can be combined to create a unique centerpiece or focal point. Decorate pillar candles by gluing leaves, glitter, stars, or anything you find interesting. Tie candles together with raffia for a unified grouping.

Clay pots make attractive candleholders and the children can personalize them with paint. For the table, try hollowed-out oranges, apples, lemons, or grapefruits as votive candle holders.

Turn the lights off and sit by candlelight and sing or talk as a family.

You may be surprised how the quiet calm of candlelight can bring sweet sanity to a very busy season.

The Wonder of Christmas

*In this lesson, we revisit, with a sense
of reverent awe, the events of the first Christmas.*

OUTLINE

If we can read the Christmas story in Luke 1 with a sense of
wonder today, it will most assuredly take on new meaning for us.
We've heard it so many times that if we are not careful, it settles
down into the comfort zone of our mental process and we lose
the sense of the incredible wonder of what happened when Christ
was born.

    I. Five Statements that Were Fulfilled

        a. The Virgin Birth

        b. The Humanity of Jesus

        c. The Messiahship of Jesus

        d. The Omnipotence of God

        e. The Deity of Jesus

    II. Two Statements Yet to Be Fulfilled

        a. The Throne of David

        b. He Shall Reign Forever

OVERVIEW

In Luke 1:26-38 we read:

> Now in the sixth month the angel Gabriel was sent by
> God to a city of Galilee named Nazareth, to a virgin
> betrothed to a man whose name was Joseph, of the
> house of David. The virgin's name was Mary. And
> having come in, the angel said to her, "Rejoice, highly
> favored one, the Lord is with you; blessed are you
> among women!" But when she saw him, she was
> troubled at his saying, and considered what manner
> of greeting this was. Then the angel said to her, "Do
> not be afraid, Mary, for you have found favor with
> God. And behold, you will conceive in your womb
> and bring forth a Son, and shall call His name
> JESUS. He will be great, and will be called the Son
> of the Highest; and the Lord God will give Him the
> throne of His father David. And He will reign over
> the house of Jacob forever, and of His kingdom there
> will be no end." Then Mary said to the angel, "How
> can this be, since I do not know a man?" And the
> angel answered and said to her, "The Holy Spirit will
> come upon you, and the power of the Highest will
> overshadow you; therefore, also, that Holy One who
> is to be born will be called the Son of God. Now
> indeed, Elizabeth your relative has also conceived a
> son in her old age; and this is now the sixth month for
> her who was called barren. For with God nothing will
> be impossible." Then Mary said, "Behold the maidser-
> vant of the Lord! Let it be to me according to your
> word." And the angel departed from her.

A young virgin named Mary is engaged to be married to a man
named Joseph. Then Mary is visited by an angel. This particular
passage is referred to as "The Annunciation." Many believe that
Luke learned the details of this story directly from Mary as he
researched the background of the gospel.

The angel Gabriel, who appeared to Mary, is one of two angels

Celebrate His Love

mentioned by name in the Bible. Michael is the great defender, while Gabriel is the great revealer. This whole dialog probably took place in Mary's home. She lived in a city of questionable reputation, yet we know she was of a pharisaic line and of royal descent. When the angel came to Mary, many people of her day were totally oblivious to any events that would have a permanent or universal influence. But one thing was true: every woman desired to become the mother of the long-awaited Messiah.

In verse 28 we read that the angel spoke to Mary and said, "Rejoice, highly favored one, the Lord is with you; blessed are you among women." This was the introduction to the message that would change the course of the world.

Perhaps no section of the gospel narrative has been more misunderstood than the words the angel spoke to Mary. When the angel said, "Rejoice, highly favored one," he was simply giving to her a greeting of great importance. In the King James Version, it is translated "full of grace." Likewise, the Latin Vulgate speaks of her as being "full of grace."

One commentator points out that "if by full of grace we mean full of grace received, then we understand the passage. But if we mean full of grace to give to others, then we have totally misapplied the words of the angel. Mary does not have grace that she bestows on others, no matter what anyone may teach."

Then the angel said, "Blessed are you among women." Elizabeth uses the same expression later on in the same chapter. "Blessed are you among women" is simply an expression that explains how Mary had been chosen from among the women to be the mother of our Lord. There is no indication that this choice was due to Mary's own worthiness. She was selected by the sovereignty of God.

"The Lord is with you," said the angel. That does not mean that at that moment conception took place miraculously. It simply conveys the idea that through this very difficult process the Lord would be with her and help her to comprehend all of the imponderables that were cast upon her that day.

And then in verses 30-31, the message of this great wonder comes home to the heart of this young woman. The angel said to her, "Do not be afraid, Mary, for you have found favor with God. And behold, you will conceive in your womb and bring forth a Son, and shall call His name JESUS." Once again, when the angel said that Mary had found favor with God, he was conveying no more than was communicated about Noah in the Old Testament, where we read that Noah found grace in the eyes of the Lord.

The Child's name is given by God, and we are told that His name is Jesus.

In verses 30 and following, seven statements that the angel gave to Mary are prophetic statements of great importance. Five of them were fulfilled when Jesus came the first time. Two of them will be fulfilled in the future.

FIVE STATEMENTS THAT WERE FULFILLED

Notice what the angel told Mary about her yet-to-be-born baby: "You will conceive in your womb." "You will . . . bring forth a Son." "You . . . shall call his name Jesus." "He will be great." And, "He . . . will be called the Son of the Highest."

Wrapped up in those first five statements by the angel to Mary are some of the greatest doctrines of the Christian faith. "You will conceive in your womb." That's the doctrine of the *virgin birth*.

"You will . . . bring forth a Son." That's the doctrine of the *humanity of Jesus*.

"You . . . shall call his name Jesus." That's the truth of His Messiahship. *He is our Messiah*.

"He will be great." That's the doctrine of the *omnipotence of God*.

And "He . . . will be called the Son of the Highest" tells us that *Jesus is Deity*.

All of these things were true of Jesus as He was born. Every prophecy of the angel to Mary was borne out in the birth of Jesus.

TWO STATEMENTS YET TO BE FULFILLED

The Bible says that yet to come are these two dimensions of our Savior: "The Lord God will give Him the throne of His father David," and, "He will reign over the house of Jacob forever, and of His kingdom there will be no end." Just as surely as the first five of those prophecies were fulfilled in the person of our Lord, you can be confident that the next two also will be fulfilled. The day is coming when *Jesus Christ will reign on the throne of His father David*; and He shall reign over the house of Jacob, and *of His kingdom there shall be no end*. It is yet future, but it will come to pass.

Isaiah the Prophet says, "Of the increase of His government and

Celebrate His Love

peace there will be no end, upon the throne of David and over His kingdom, to order it and establish it with judgment and justice from that time forward, even forever" (Isaiah 9:7). Jesus Christ who came in a manger will someday come in glory.

Now put yourself for a moment into the heart and mind and spirit of Mary. She is perhaps 16 years old. In that day, girls often were married at the age of 14 and had given birth by the time they were 15 or 16. So perhaps at the age of 16 or 17 she heard this overwhelming message from an angel, and then had to absorb it all.

We should have no difficulty comprehending her confusion. Verse 29 says, "When she saw him, she was troubled at his saying." That has to be one of the great understatements of the New Testament! She was perplexed. The angel's words awakened in her a sense of wonder and uneasiness, and she began to wonder what this could mean. In verse 29 she considered what manner of greeting this was.

And then she begins to ask the normal questions. These are the questions you would expect her to ask. Her first one is, how can this be? "Then Mary said to the angel, 'How can this be, since I do not know a man?'" (Luke 1:34). She is not talking about casual acquaintance here. This is the New Testament word for a sexual relationship. She is saying, "How can I be pregnant when I have not had any sexual relationship with a man?"

The angel said to her, "The Holy Spirit will come upon you, and the power of the Highest will overshadow you; therefore, also, that Holy One who is to be born will be called the Son of God" (Luke 1:35). In other words, "Mary, you are going to be with child in a way that no one has ever been with child before, or shall ever be afterwards." She will be with child by the Holy Spirit.

There are many ways humanity has come into being. Adam and Eve were created directly by God. They did not come through the birth process. Today, we are the products of a relationship between our mother and our father. But Jesus was uniquely born in the sense that He was born of His mother, but had no earthly father. So Mary was asked, at the age of 16, to comprehend a concept, a birth process, that had never before occurred in the history of humanity. No wonder she was perplexed!

This is the glory and the wonder of Christmas, that God could plant not only into the womb of this woman the Son of God, but He could plant in her heart the faith to believe the message that she received from the angel. Her response has always overwhelmed me with a sense of absolute submission that ought to be in the heart of every child of God. Mary said, "Behold the maidservant of the Lord! Let it be to me according to your word."

In one of his writings, C. S. Lewis said: "The whole thing narrows and narrows until at last it comes down to a little point, small as the point of a spear: A Jewish girl at her prayers. Today as I read the accounts of Jesus' birth, I tremble to think of the fate of the world resting on the response of two rural teenagers. How many times did Mary review the angel's words as she felt the Son of God kicking against the walls of her uterus? How many times did Joseph second guess his own encounter with an angel—just a dream?—as he endured the hot shame of living among villagers who could plainly see the changing shape of his fiancé."

The Virgin Mary, whose parenthood was unplanned, heard the angel out, pondered the repercussions, and replied: "I am the Lord's servant. May it be to me as you have said." Often a work of God comes with two edges, great joy and great pain. In this matter-of-fact response, Mary embraced both pain and joy. She was the first person to accept Jesus on His own terms, regardless of personal cost. She accepted Him as her baby.

The wonder of Christmas!

We should be overwhelmed that God should love us so much, that Christ His Son would allow Himself to be born into humanity to ultimately pay the penalty for our sin.

APPLICATION

1. Based on your understanding of Jewish culture, what response to her unwed pregnancy might Mary have expected from the community around her?

Where, in Luke 1:46-55, does she project what others will call her in the future? What does this reveal about Mary's spirit and attitude?

2. What does Luke 2:19 reveal about Mary's perspective on the events surrounding Jesus' conception and birth?

   Why was this remarkable?

3. What word does Mary use to describe herself in Luke 1:38 and in Luke 1:48?

   Does this seem to confirm or contradict other aspects of her character?

   How does this compare or contrast with the view of Mary held by some religious groups?

4. Why do you think Joseph and Mary did not "go public" with the news of the angelic visits? In addition to Mary's humiliation, what might Joseph have had to endure?

What attitude do you think made it possible for them to do this?

5. What was Simeon's attitude concerning the arrival of Messiah, according to Luke 2:29-32? How did Joseph and Mary respond to his statements?

6. How might we respond to the season celebrating His birth, in light of the responses of those closest to Him at His birth?

DID YOU KNOW?

Because the timetable for the arrival of Messiah is so precise in Daniel 9:25-26, there were some during the days leading up to Jesus' birth who were faithfully watching for Messiah's birth somewhere near the "69 weeks" (483 years) following the decree of Artaxerxes found in Nehemiah 2:1-8 (made in 444 B.C.). But that also meant there were a multitude of imposters trying to cash in on Daniel's prophecy by claiming to be the Messiah.

God's solution to the problem of imposters was to provide a multitude of qualifications Messiah would have to meet—including genealogical criteria, the ability to effect Messianic signs, a sinless life, and ultimately power over Satan and death itself. And, although most (if not all) believing Jews did not foresee the death and resurrection of Messiah, once it was all accomplished, they could write with great wonder and awe about the perfection of God's plan as it unfolded in Jesus the Messiah. Thus the New Testament is filled to the brim with quotations and allusions to the Old Testament prophecies fulfilled in the Babe born at Bethlehem.

Star of Wonder

Atop many a Christmas tree is the Christmas Star. To most Christians it is a symbol of Jesus, who is often called the 'bright and morning star.' Ancient people looked upon stars as gods and created myths about them. Before there was Christmas, stars held importance in ancient religions.

The Babylonians used three stars to represent a god. The Egyptians believed that certain gods controlled different stars and constellations. The six-pointed star of David became the symbol of the Hebrew nation. The North American Blackfoot Indian tribe believed that every star at one time was a human being. But the five-pointed star of Christmas holds center stage. Its appearance is recorded in the Bible in the New Testament, which says it appeared over Bethlehem and served as a guiding light to lead the wise men to the Holy Child.

Wondering at the Baby

*In this lesson we narrow our focus
to the Baby born at Bethlehem, examining the miraculous
and wonder-inspiring factors surrounding Jesus' birth.*

OUTLINE

During the hectic weeks and days of the holiday season, we may talk about the merchandising, and the caroling, and the festivities and the programs and the pageants, and in the process sometimes, even of all the good things—but we lose the wonder of the season. And to lose the wonder of the season is to lose our wonder at the Baby whose birth is commemorated at this time of year.

   I. Let Us Wonder at His Birth

  II. Let Us Wonder at His Human Family

  II. Let Us Wonder at His Hostile Rejection

 III. Let Us Wonder at His Hated Worshipers

 IV. Let Us Wonder at His Holy Mission

OVERVIEW

From Eugene Peterson's paraphrase of the New Testament Scriptures, *The Message*, Luke 2 reads:

> About that time, Caesar Augustus ordered a census to be taken throughout the Empire. This was the first census when Quirinius was governor of Syria. Everyone had to travel to his own ancestral home-town to be accounted for. So Joseph went from the Galilean town of Nazareth up to Bethlehem in Judah, David's town, for the census. As a descendant of David, he had to go there. He went with Mary, his fiancée, who was pregnant. While they were there, the time came for her to give birth. She gave birth to a son, her firstborn. She wrapped him in a blanket and laid him in a manger, because there was no room in the hostel.
>
> There were sheepherders camping in the neigh-borhood. They had set night watches over their sheep. Suddenly God's angel stood among them and God's glory blazed around them. They were terrified. The angel said, "Don't be afraid. I'm here to announce a great and joyful event that is meant for everybody, worldwide. A Savior has just been born in David's town, a Savior who is Messiah and Master. This is what you are to look for: a baby wrapped in a blanket and lying in a manger." At once the angel was joined by a huge angelic choir singing God's praises: "Glory to God in the heavenly heights. Peace to all men and women on earth who please him."
>
> As the angel choir withdrew to heaven, the sheepherders talked it over. "Let's go over to Bethlehem as fast as we can and see for ourselves what God has revealed to us." They left, running, and found Mary and Joseph, and the baby lying in the manger. Seeing was believing. They told everyone they met what the angels had said about this child. All who heard the sheepherders were impressed.

The King James says it this way: "And all they that heard it wondered." They wondered at the story.

The date was December 17, 1903. The place was Kittyhawk, North Carolina. Orville and Wilbur Wright had just made history by keeping their flying invention in the air for a total of 59 seconds. Elated, they rushed to the telegraph office and wired their sister in Dayton, Ohio. Here was the telegram: "First sustained flight today for 59 seconds," the message read. "Hope to be home by Christmas." Their sister was thrilled, and she hurried to the local newspaper with the great news and the telegram. And sure enough, the next day there was an article about the Wrights in the Dayton Daily News. The headline read, "Local Bicycle Merchants to be Home for the Holidays." Not one thing was mentioned about the first airplane flight that anyone ever took.

When I read that story earlier this year I thought, "Isn't that like Christmas?" We give all the details and we forget the wonder, the most important message of all. For just a little while this year, I have captured that wonder in a way that I cannot remember for a long time. I cannot tell you why it is, but I know that what I have sensed in my heart about all of this, I wish I could package up and convey.

LET US WONDER AT HIS BIRTH

Born in Bethlehem. Jesus was born in the meekest and most unobtrusive of places.

History tells us that early in the nineteenth century, the whole world was watching the campaigns of Napoleon. There was talk everywhere of marches, invasions, battles, and bloodshed as the French dictator pushed his way through Europe. Of course, babies were born during that time. But who had time to think about babies or to care about cradles or nurseries when the international scene was as tumultuous as it was? Nevertheless, between Trafalgar and Waterloo there stole into this world a veritable host of heroes whose lives were destined to shape all of humanity.

Take, for example, William Gladstone, born in 1809. Gladstone was destined to become one of the finest statesmen England produced.

Also in 1809, Alfred Tennyson was born to an obscure minister and his wife. Tennyson would one day greatly affect the literary world in a marked manner.

Oliver Wendell Holmes was born in Cambridge, Massachusetts, in 1809.

Not far away in Boston, Edgar Allen Poe began his eventful but tragic life.

It was also in that same year that a physician named Darwin and his wife named their child Charles Robert.

And it was that same year that the cries of a newborn infant could be heard from a rugged log cabin in Harlan County, Kentucky. The baby's name was Abraham Lincoln.

If there had been news broadcasts at that time, I am certain these words would have been heard. "The destiny of the world is being shaped on an Austrian battlefield today." But today, only a handful of history buffs can name even two of the three Austrian campaigns. Looking back, history was actually being shaped in the cradles of England and America as young mothers held in their arms the movers and shakers of the future.

It was that way with Jesus. No one heralded His coming. The shepherds, the angels, the Magi, a few would-be worshipers. Had you written the story of that year, you would have said, "Nothing really important happened this year." But that year, the Savior of the world was born, in that humble place called Bethlehem, where Deity would invade eternity, where eternity would invade time, and where royalty would come dressed up as poverty. Only God could have written such a script! Who could have thought of such a humble story for the entrance of our Lord?

LET US WONDER AT HIS HUMAN FAMILY

I say that advisedly because His family was really a human mother and one who was a stand-in father, for Jesus was conceived of the Holy Spirit. But consider his human family: Mary, 15 or 16 years of age; Joseph no more than 19; a young, unassuming couple. Yet into their family was to be born the Savior of the world.

The most significant event of the centuries took place in a stable in an insignificant city called Bethlehem. I cannot help but wonder what Mary thought. What went through her mind as she saw that little One? The most significant thing in the history of the world did not happen in Caesar's court, or in the palace, or in the plans of the Jewish zealots. The most significant thing happened in a manger. As

Mary held that Baby, I wonder if she heard ringing in her ears the words of Isaiah the Prophet: "Therefore the Lord Himself will give you a sign: Behold, the virgin shall conceive and bear a Son, and shall call His name Immanuel" (Isaiah 7:14). Mary held Immanuel in her arms. Do we wonder at that? Is that not an awesome thing, that the Savior of the world would be born in such a way?

Let Us Wonder at His Hostile Rejection

The Scriptures record that when they came to Bethlehem, it was an unheralded arrival. There were no signs pointing to the coming of the Messiah. There was no welcome party there to receive Him. In fact, since it was the time of census, there was no place for anyone to stay. Roman soldiers had come to occupy the town to administer the census, so when Mary and Joseph came (while the record does not tell us), it is quite probable that they had tried all of the places along the way. And finally there was nowhere else for them to go. So the innkeeper simply had to say, "We have no place." Perhaps they could clean out a corner of the stable and at least provide a shelter for this birth.

Let Us Wonder at His Hated Worshipers

The Scriptures tell us that those who gathered to worship Him first were shepherds. In our culture, that loses some of its meaning, and therefore some of its wonder. In that time and culture, however, shepherds would be the last and least to expect the Prince of Peace to come to them. They were shepherds. They were ceremonially unclean. They were not allowed to go into the temple area to worship. They were unaccepted. They were nobodies. They could not be called as witnesses in court, for somebody had written that no one could believe the testimony of a shepherd. They were despised. They were looked down upon and often hated. The Jewish Talmud says of them, "Give no help to a heathen or to a shepherd." That's how they were appreciated. What a wonder, that God would choose them to witness the birth of His Son, to be there first to worship the coming of the Messiah. The shepherds!

Out of the whole of Jewish society, He chose shepherds. Out of the entire population of Jerusalem and Bethlehem, these outcasts were the only ones who came to see the Messiah and to spread the news of His coming.

This is really the only thing that brings wonder to the rest of the story. Apart from His mission, this is just a good seasonal tale. But when we put all of these things together, and then understand that the purpose for all of this was that He might come to be our Redeemer, we cannot help but be in awe. His purpose in coming was to die—to die for you and for me.

We can sum it up this way:

The Creator in a cradle.

The Savior in a stable.

The Messiah of the world in a mother's womb.

The Sovereign of history welcomed by shepherds on a hillside.

The Lion of the Tribe of Judah as Mary's little Lamb.

The Lord of Glory lying upon the straw.

I cannot get my arms around it. It is too wonderful.

He was the Savior of the world, the most awesome person who ever walked on this earth. This is the wonder of Christ.

So how do we express our wonder? It's not fair to inspire such wonder without talking about how we do it.

We need to discipline ourselves to do it. It won't happen unless we say, "This is my time with the Lord. This is my time to wonder at Christmas and what He has done for me." And if we will do that, this will not be just another Christmas season. The wonder of this incredible message will explode upon our hearts. It may cause the irrigation of our eyes. But it will certainly put warmth in our breast and hope in our heart.

1. Read all of Luke, chapters 1-2, adding up the total number of people who apparently recognized who Jesus really was. Do you think this kind of inconspicuous arrival is what the Jews were expecting?

   Why do you think God did it this way?

2. From a purely human standpoint, what kinds of things might have been said about Joseph and Mary's little family as Jesus was growing up?

   What most certainly would not have been said about them, particularly in light of Israel's hope for a Messiah?

3. From what we know about the Herods who ruled over Judea during Jesus' birth and childhood, what would they have done to a child proclaimed to be the future King of Kings?

What does this help us understand?

4. Why do you think so little of Jesus' childhood is recorded?

How does John 1:11 help explain this?

5. How do the following passages add to our wonderment at the birth of Jesus?
   a. John 1:1-3, 14

   b. Colossians 1:9

   c. Philippians 2:6-11

   d. Isaiah 9:6-7

DID YOU KNOW?

Though the genealogical requirements of the coming Messiah were specifically outlined in the Old Testament and carefully documented in the Temple archives, teachers in the years leading up to Jesus' birth had a problem. While 2 Samuel 7:12-17 clearly indicated that the Messiah must (1) come from David's own body, and (2) inherit the throne of Israel through Solomon's line, God's curse on wicked King Jeconiah (also called Jehoiachin and Coniah) in Jeremiah 22:30 seemed to indicate that no one in the royal line of David through Solomon actually could rule as Messiah over Israel.

That's why God provides for us two genealogies of Jesus. The one in Luke 3 traces Jesus' physical line through Heli (Mary's father) back to David's own body, not through Solomon, but through David's son, Nathan. And the one in Matthew 1 traces Jesus' legal right to the throne through his legal adoptive father Joseph, who was in the legal line of Solomon—but who, by virtue of the virgin birth of Jesus, did not father Jesus, and thus did not violate God's curse on Jeconiah's physical descendants.

Complicated? A little—but (wonder of wonders!) it shows that Jesus was the only Person in all of human history who could fulfill the genealogical requirements of Messiahship!

A Place for Baby Jesus

Establish the priority of Jesus' birthday as the focus of this season of celebration by making your first holiday activity the placement of a nativity scene in your home. It may be as simple as a paper fold-out—or as elaborate as life-size figures on your front lawn. Determine a place for the Holy Family and make it a family event to usher in the Christmas season. Young children learn priorities by what you do, not what you say.

Immanuel

*In this lesson we consider the miraculous nature of
"Immanuel" — the very presence of God in human form,
incarnated as a Baby in Bethlehem.*

OUTLINE

The real story of Christmas is God becoming a man so that He could
reveal Himself and reveal His love to all mankind. It is the very
essence of the Gospel. It is the glad tidings of great joy which the
angels spoke about on the hillside outside of Bethlehem.

   I. The Mystery of Immanuel

  II. The Meaning of Immanuel

     a. We Have the Confidence to Face the Challenges of Life

     b. We Are Certain that Our Prayers Are Heard and
       Understood

     c. We Have the Courage to Serve Him in Difficult Places

Seldom is this truth ever discussed at Christmastime. Yet it is one of the central doctrines of the Word of God. John the Apostle wrote in John 1:14: "And the Word became flesh and dwelt among us, and we beheld His glory, the glory as of the only begotten of the Father, full of grace and truth."

In what some consider to be a hymn from the early church, we read of this great mystery in the Book of Philippians: "Let this mind be in you which was also in Christ Jesus, who, being in the form of God, did not consider it robbery to be equal with God, but made Himself of no reputation, taking the form of a bond-servant, and coming in the likeness of men. And being found in appearance as a man, He humbled Himself and became obedient to the point of death, even the death of the cross" (Philippians 2:5-8).

And writing in more formal tones in the Book of Galatians, Paul put it this way: "But when the fullness of the time had come, God sent forth His Son, born of a woman, born under the law" (Galatians 4:4).

The Prophet Isaiah predicted that the day would come when God would visit His people just like this; that the Son of God would come and confine Himself to a human body; and that His sacrificial love in doing that would forever remind them of His great compassion for their lost estate. Isaiah prophesied, "Therefore the Lord Himself will give you a sign: Behold, the virgin shall conceive and bear a Son, and shall call His name Immanuel" (Isaiah 7:14).

And Matthew, in his gospel narrative of the birth of Christ, picked up what Isaiah had prophesied, and used it in application to the Lord Jesus. Listen to his words: "Behold, the virgin shall be with child, and bear a Son, and they shall call His name Immanuel, which is translated, 'God with us'" (Matthew 1:23).

There is an old poet who has presented the Son of God as having the stars for His crown, and the sky for His mantle, and the clouds for His bow, and the fire for His spear. And he rode forth in His majestic robes of glory, but one day He resolved in conference with His Father that He would come to earth, and He shed all of His clothes on the way. The stars were gone, the sky was gone, the clouds were divested. When He was asked what He would wear when He got to the earth, He replied with a smile that He had new clothes in the making down below, and those clothes were the clothes of humanity, the robes of flesh and blood. And with this new wardrobe He was given a new name, and that name was Immanuel.

Of all the names of the Lord Jesus that were given to Him for His time on this earth, this one is my favorite. His name is Immanuel, which being translated is "God with us."

As Christians, we sometimes feel that in order to really appreciate our faith, we need to understand everything about it. But the more I study the Gospel, the more I become aware of the vastness of truth that I do not comprehend. The one thing I will never comprehend is God becoming a man. But I must not put myself in a corner and say that in order for me to appreciate and believe it, I must completely comprehend it. There always must be something mysterious about the God who created the heavens and the earth. Paul seemed almost overcome by the thought of it when writing to his young friend Timothy. In 1 Timothy 3:16 he wrote, "And without controversy, great is the mystery of godliness: God was manifested in the flesh." Paul was saying to young Timothy, "I can't explain this. But let me just tell you this. There is no controversy at all about it. Without controversy, great is the mystery."

Isn't it wonderful to be able to pause for a moment and reflect on the mystery and the wonder of our God? Wondering at the Christ Child. Wondering at Immanuel. Wondering at God manifested in the flesh. God became a man—like your neighbor, like you, like me.

Writer after writer has tried to help us understand the majestic mystery of God manifested in the flesh. For instance, C. S. Lewis, in *Mere Christianity*, wrote these words: "The second person in God, the Son, became human Himself: was born into the world as an actual man—a real man of a particular height, with hair of a particular color, speaking a particular language, weighing so many pounds. The Eternal Being, who knows everything and who created the whole universe, became not only a man but (before that) a baby, and before that a fetus inside a woman's body."

A. W. Tozer, the great Alliance preacher, was also overwhelmed by this thought. He wrote: "The coming of Jesus Christ into this world represents a truth more profound than any philosophy. All of the great thinkers of the world together could never have produced anything even remotely approaching the wonder and profundity disclosed in the message of these words . . . He came . . . The words are wiser than all learning. Understood in their high spiritual context, they are more eloquent than all oratory, more lyric and moving than all music. They tell us that all of mankind, sitting in darkness, has been visited by the Light of the World!"

Finally, Frederick Buechner adds, "The claim that Christianity makes for Christmas is that at a particular time and place God came to be with us Himself. When Quirinius was governor of Syria, in a town called Bethlehem, a child was born who, beyond the power of anyone to account for, was the high and lofty One made low and helpless. The One who inhabits eternity comes to dwell in time. The One whom none can look upon and live—is delivered in a stable under the soft, indifferent gaze of cattle. The Father of all mercies puts Himself at our mercy."

If one of us were God, is that the way we would have done it? Would we have made that plan to rescue lost mankind? Would we have sent the Redeemer in a manger, wrapped in strips of swaddling cloth? Would we have had Him born in a stable built for animals? Would we have had His first visitors be the hated shepherds of the hillside? It is a mystery beyond mysteries, a story written by the finger of God, and one that we will never comprehend. But it is also one that we should always appreciate.

THE MEANING OF IMMANUEL

The reason why Immanuel is such a precious name to all of us who know Him is that we understand the meaning of it. We may never comprehend the mystery of it, but we understand the meaning of it. God with us.

God is not distant. He is here, with us. He is not unapproachable, unreachable. He has reached down to us through His Son, the Lord Jesus. He has revealed Himself to us in the only kind of persons we know—human persons. He became one of us so that we could know Him, so that we could know how much He loves us.

What Christmas reveals to us is that we have a God who has condescended in the midst of our suffering, and He has come to help us and share with us and enable us to face it and conquer it. The Christmas name of our Lord reminds us of this wonderful truth: His name shall be called Immanuel. God with us.

We Have the Confidence to Face the Challenges of Life

We all face challenges in life, and we are so wonderfully blessed to be able to open the Bible and read there of a Savior who has come to be one of us. And because He is with us, He is able to encourage us in every manner of test and challenge we may ever face. Consider:

- Hebrews 13:5-6: "Let your conduct be without covetousness; and be content with such things as you have. For He Himself has said, 'I will never leave you nor forsake you.' So we may boldly say, 'The Lord is my helper; I will not fear. What can man do to me?'"
- Psalm 27:1: "The LORD is my light and my salvation. Whom shall I fear? The LORD is the strength of my life; Of whom shall I be afraid?"
- Psalm 118:6: "The LORD is on my side, I will not fear; What can man do to me?"
- Isaiah 43:2-3: "When you pass through the waters, I will be with you; and through the rivers, they shall not overflow you. When you walk through the fire, you shall not be burned, nor shall the flame scorch you. For I am the LORD your God, the Holy One of Israel, your Savior. I gave Egypt for your ransom, Ethiopia and Seba in your place."

God with us. Because God is with us, we have the confidence to face the challenges of life.

We Are Certain that Our Prayers are Heard and Understood

Sometimes, if we do not know what the Bible says, we wonder if God really even comprehends what we are praying. Aren't you glad that when you pray you have someone who hears and understands you and knows what you feel? Why does Christ know that? Because the One to whom you address your prayers is Immanuel, the One who is God with us.

Listen to what the Book of Hebrews says concerning Immanuel: "For we do not have a High Priest who cannot sympathize with our weaknesses, but was in all points tempted as we are, yet without sin. Let us therefore come boldly to the throne of grace, that we may obtain mercy and find grace to help in time of need" (Hebrews 4:15-16).

When you go to the Lord God in prayer through Jesus Christ, and you tell Him your need, He is Immanuel who has been in every place you have been. He knows every need you have. He knows every burden you bear. He knows every sorrow you have felt. And He has borne those burdens and those sorrows to their ultimate. And you can pray with confidence because He is Immanuel.

We Have the Courage to Serve Him in Difficult Places

How do you continue to serve God? Of course, some might say, "What do you mean? I'm not in the ministry." But the truth is that every Christian is in the ministry. You may not be formally ordained, but if you are a Christian, you are serving God. (And if you are not serving God, why aren't you?)

Every believer serves God. And some serve God in some very difficult places. The place God has called us to serve is 90 percent pagan. The place where God has called us to serve puts us in an extreme minority. No one else gives any credence to our faith, yet we have been called of God to serve there.

Christianity is not about religion. It is about a relationship. If you have a relationship with Jesus Christ and you are serving Him in a tough place, my friend, you better know Immanuel. Because you can't do that by yourself. You have to have God with you. It has always been that way.

When God spoke to Moses and told him that he was being commissioned to lead the people out of Egypt, Moses had all kinds of excuses. Remember all of that list of excuses he gave to God. But listen to what God said to him in Exodus 4:12: "Go, and I will be with your mouth, and teach you what you shall say."

Moses got them out of Egypt, then it was time for Joshua to get them into Canaan. They were going to have to face the giants of the land of Canaan, the most pagan people of that time. Obviously Joshua was frightened. But he got his commission from God in Joshua 1:9: "Have I not commanded you? Be strong and of good courage; do not be afraid, nor be dismayed, for the LORD your God is with you wherever you go."

He is the Immanuel who goes with you when you have been

called to serve in a tough place.

And then there was Jeremiah, commissioned to go to a stubborn people with a message of judgment. Every time I read that book of the Bible, I am encouraged about everything God has ever asked me to do. God told Jeremiah to preach judgment to people who would not only not listen, but would not do one single thing he ever told them to do. God said, "Go preach to them. Tell them what I've told you to tell them. But know up front that they are not going to listen, they are not going to do anything about it, and they are going to scoff at you while you preach."

Jeremiah went into that scenario with that commission—but then God said to him in Jeremiah 1:8, "'Do not be afraid of their faces, for I am with you to deliver you,' says the LORD."

All of us have been commissioned as disciples to go into the world and preach the gospel. And what is it that the Lord says to all of us who do that? In Matthew 28:20 He says, ". . . lo, I am with you always, even to the end of the age."

Because God is with us, we have confidence to face the challenges of life; we don't go alone. We have certainty that our prayers are heard and understood because God has been where we are. And we have the courage to serve Him no matter how difficult the task may be.

1. List any famous people (sports stars, media celebrities, politicians, etc.) you have met during your life. How did you act around them?

    How would you respond if they dropped by your house?

    How many other people did you inform about your meeting or acquaintance?

2. Compare your answers to the previous question to your actions, response, and words as someone who has met the God of the universe. Is it a good comparison, or something less?

Is there room for change in light of knowing the "God with us," Jesus Christ?

3. In Exodus 40:34, what was the purpose of the tabernacle (tent) of the Lord, which was set up in the middle of all the tents of Israel?

How does this connect with John 1:14, which says literally that the Word became flesh and dwelled among us?

4. If Jesus was the "Seed of woman" promised in Genesis 3:15, who did He come to ultimately defeat?

Why couldn't this be done by a mortal human being?

When will this conquest be completed?

5. What does 1 John 5:19 reveal about the present condition of the world?

Was this true when Christ was born?

Then why couldn't Satan defeat Him?

What does I John 4:4 reveal about the present condition of each believer, and the similarities to Christ's entrance into the world?

6. Read Daniel 7:9-10, 13-14. What is the eventual position of the Son?

Compare this to Isaiah 9:6-7. Why do you think He was not revealed in this way when He came as a Baby to Bethlehem?

When will He be?

DID YOU KNOW?

Christianity is unique among the world's religions in proposing that there is no way that man can, through anything he does, ever reach God; but that God, in His infinite love and mercy, became man in order to rescue any who would be rescued.

This concept not only is foreign to the world's religions, but in Islam is considered to be blasphemy. Nowhere is this more vividly displayed than in the Arabic statement emblazoned on the outside of the Dome of the Rock, which stands over the location of the Holy of Holies on the Temple Mount in Jerusalem.

It reads: "Allah is God, Allah is One. He was not born, nor did He beget."

Hence the hopelessness of those who do not recognize Immanuel, "God With Us."

Celebrate His Love

The Hanging of the Greens

The evergreen nature of conifers and hollies has long made them symbols of eternal life through Christ Jesus. Red berries are used as a symbol of Christ's blood, which was shed for us.

Early in December each year, our congregation participates in readying our sanctuary for a season of celebration.

We usually use pine branch "roping" to make swags, and evergreen wreaths as our focal points.

You Shall Call His Name "Jesus"

In this lesson we focus on the name "Jesus" and its significance for us as believers today.

OUTLINE

What's in a name? Jesus is called by His name 500 times in the gospels. In the New Testament the name Jesus appears 909 times. It is obviously the most endearing and most loved name for our Savior. And, as we will find out, it is packed with meaning and significance.

   I. Jesus Is Pronounced the Same in Almost Every Language

  II. Jesus Is an Esteemed Name

 III. Jesus Is an Enduring Name

 IV. Jesus Is an Exalted Name

  V. Jesus Is an Exclusive Name

There are at least 562 names for Jesus in the Bible.

If we study how people name their children, and if we go way back, we discover that often children were named for their fathers. That's why we have common names in the English language like Thompson, Johnson, Peterson, and Jackson. That practice was fairly common in New Testament times as well.

Sometimes people received a name based on a role that they would bear for the family. Their name reflected the hope that was wrapped up in the child.

Sometimes a name would be given just because of preference. We do that today when we use those little books with all the names of girls and boys in them.

But when an Old Testament Hebrew named his child, he did so with great thought. Hebrew children were named carefully because they bore some special message within the family. An Orthodox Jew would never glibly decide the name of his child. So as God sent His Son into the world to be clothed with humanity, He would need to give Him a meaningful name.

How would He do it? What would He call Him? He would not leave it up to the human parents to choose. It was so important that this name be right that God originated it and brought the message down to earth by means of an angel. The angel delivered the name to Mary's husband. The record of that conversation is in Matthew 1:21. The Bible says that the angel spoke to Joseph and said to him, "And she [Mary] will bring forth a Son and you shall call His name JESUS, for He will save His people from their sins" (Matthew 1:21). By special instruction expressing God's will, it came to pass in Bethlehem, that when the Child was born and someone said, "Who is He and what is His name?" the answer was clearly given: His name is Jesus.

One interesting thing you can do if you have the opportunity is to glance through a hymn book and see how hymn writers have memorialized this name so we can worship using the name of Jesus. John Newton gave us, "How Sweet the Name of Jesus Sounds." Edward Perronet exalts this name with, "All Hail the Power of Jesus' Name." Bernard of Clairvaux leads us in an old hymn called, "Jesus, the Very Thought of Thee." Lydia Baxter gave us, "Take the Name of Jesus with You." And Frederick Whitfield adds, "There is a Name I Love to Hear."

It is a wonderful name that our Father gave to His Son, a combination of two words, put together to mean, "Jehovah Saves." Salvation, you see, was the expressed purpose of Jesus' coming into the world. And if a name is to call forth the primary character wrapped up in the person, then Jesus could not have been better named, for He was here for one purpose, and that was to bring salvation to lost men and women.

Let's think for a moment about the fact that "Jesus" is an easy name.

JESUS IS PRONOUNCED THE SAME IN ALMOST EVERY LANGUAGE

The name Jesus has only two syllables and five letters. It is pronounced the same in almost every language. I love to listen to missionary stations on short wave radio, and often, even though I don't understand the language, I will be able to pick the name "Jesus" out of the lyrics of a foreign language. There is something symmetrical about it in almost every language. It is a name which is known around the world, yet even a child can learn it.

If you carry that name into all the languages and dialects of the world, whether Hebrew or Greek or Anglo-Saxon, you can translate it—but you can never rob it of its music. Its tones break in upon your ear when you hear it. There is no word that is sweeter to a person who is a Christian than the word "Jesus."

God said to the angel, "We shall call Him Jesus," and that name was registered in heaven for the Son of God.

Bernard of Clairvaux expressed our heart when he wrote these words which we still sing often today:

> *Jesus, the very thought of Thee.*
> *No voice can sing, no heart can frame,*
> *Nor can the memory find*
> *A sweeter sound than Thy blest name,*
> *O Savior of mankind.*

The Christmas name of our Lord is, first and foremost, the name Jesus. Jesus is an easy name.

According to Josephus, there are eleven men in the Old Testament who have the name Joshua, the Old Testament equivalent of Jesus. No Old Testament parents had ever called their child Joshua until one day Moses was renaming some men. They were men who were going to go in and spy out the land, and in Numbers 13:16 we read these words: "These are the names of the men whom Moses sent to spy out the land. And Moses called Hoshea, the son of Nun, Joshua." Moses gave him a new name, and that name is the same name we would call Jesus in the New Testament. It means "Jehovah Saves."

There are many Bible scholars who believe Joshua is an Old Testament picture of Jesus. And there are some wonderful points of resemblance in this way. Joshua led the Israelites out of the wilderness into the Promised Land. Jesus, as our Savior, brings us out of the wilderness of sin into the spiritual Promised Land.

Joshua led his people to conquest over their enemies and their walled cities and their tall giants. Jesus leads us to conquest over the enemies of our soul, and helps us to fight against life's difficult giants of temptation and trial and testing. As our Joshua, Jesus leads us to the inheritance that God has promised us.

But obviously the Jesus of the New Testament far transcends anything we can say about Joshua in the Old. In fact, in Hebrews 4:8 the writer of Hebrews says this: "For if Joshua had given them rest, then he would not afterward have spoken of another day." In other words, if Joshua could have provided the victory which we truly need in the Old Testament sense of the word, there wouldn't have been any need of another Joshua. But Joshua could only do that which was temporal, only that which was earth-bound, only that which is for our physical well-being. But Jesus came to do something eternal. He didn't just come to free us from slavery and lead us out of the wilderness into a new land. He came to give us life everlasting. That's why our Jesus is better than Joshua. It's an esteemed name.

JESUS IS AN ENDURING NAME

He was given that name over 2,000 years ago, yet His name today is the most well-known name in all the world. No other person has a name as well-known as the name of Jesus. This season of the year always intrigues me, because those who are absolutely in conflict with Jesus, those who don't want anything to do with Him, who use that name as a swear word, those who defy everything we try to do in the name of evangelism, those who are enemies of Jesus—they all come to His birthday party. If you want evidence for the power of the name of Jesus, you don't need a Bible, you don't need a preacher. Just watch what happens during the Christmas season. Jesus has an enduring name.

JESUS IS AN EXALTED NAME

His name is an exalted name. Ephesians 1:20-21 reads, ". . . which He [God] worked in Christ when He raised Him from the dead and seated Him at His right hand in the heavenly places far above all principality and power and might and dominion, and every name that is named, not only in this age but also in that which is to come." How exalted is His name? It is far above every name that has been named, or that ever will be named. It is the highest name of all names in all the world for all time. It is the number one name.

Paul wrote in Philippians 2:9-11, "Therefore God also has highly exalted Him and given Him the name which is above every name, that at the name of Jesus every knee should bow, of those in heaven and those on earth, and of those under the earth, and that every tongue should confess that Jesus is Lord, to the glory of God the Father."

Paul said it as well as it could be said. The name of Jesus is the most important name in all the world. It is an exalted name.

JESUS IS AN EXCLUSIVE NAME

Jesus' name is different from any other name. The angel told Joseph the reason when he spoke to him and gave him that name: "And she shall bring forth a Son and you shall call His name JESUS, for He will save His people from their sins" (Matthew 1:21). Jesus has an exclusive name because the purpose of that name was to stamp forever upon His personality the uniqueness of His mission. What was His mission? Jesus means "Jehovah Saves." What was the uniqueness about Jesus? He was the one who would come into the world to be the Savior of lost mankind. That is why He was called Jesus. Exclusively, one of a kind. There never has been, nor will there ever be anyone who can do what Jesus came to do.

I love to tell that story. I love for people to understand that this unique person of all the universe was the only hope of lost mankind, for He was the only God-man. He was God reaching down for man because God could not reach up to God. And in Him is salvation.

That is why the writer of the Book of Acts says, "Nor is there salvation in any other for there is no other name under heaven given among men by which we must be saved"(Acts 4:12). That's the only name. Do you want to go to heaven? You have to go through the name of Jesus. It is exclusive.

Jesus does for you what no one else can do. The Lord Jesus Christ changes a person from the inside out and makes them new.

Do you know Him? We go through all these celebrations, and parties and gift giving and decorating our homes and celebrating the Christmas season. There are certain times in the year where I just have such an incredible burden to be as simple as I can be about what it means to know God. It means to know His Son, Jesus Christ, as your Savior.

My friends, Jesus can do for you what nobody else can do. Your wife or your husband can't do it. Your children can't do it. Your parents can't do it. Your teacher can't do it. Your pastor can't do it. But Jesus can. He came into the world, born of a virgin, the uniquely born Son of God, God walking around in a body, and His Father said, "Call Him Jesus, for He is going to save His people from their sins."

He went to the cross, hung there between heaven and earth, and paid the penalty for your sin and mine. He fulfilled the prophecy that His Father has spoken of Him when He named Him. And today He is in heaven at the right hand of the Father making intercession for those who believe in Him.

If you have never put your trust in the name of Jesus and in the Jesus of the name, then you must do it. Without Him there is no hope, there is no future, there is no meaning in this life. He came to give you what you cannot get any place else—forgiveness for your sin and the assurance of eternal life.

1. What attributes of God are connected with the name of Jesus in the following passages?

   a. Ephesians 3:9

   b. Philippians 2:10-11

   c. 2 Thessalonians 1:7

   d. Hebrews 13:8

   e. 1 John 2:1

2. What benefits for every believer are connected with His name in the passages below?

   a. Romans 5:15

   b. Romans 8:2

   c. 1 Corinthians 15:57

   d. 2 Corinthians 5:18

   e. Galatians 3:26

   f. Ephesians 2:13

   g. Philippians 3:14

   h. 1 Thessalonians 5:9

Celebrate His Love

3. What kinds of responses, actions, and words did the name of Jesus stimulate during the earliest years of the church, according to the passages below?

   a. Acts 9:29

   b. Acts 15:25-26

   c. Acts 19:17

   d. Acts 21:13

   e. Acts 26:9-10

4. In light of Acts 4:12, how would you respond to a statement like, "Jesus is just another name for the same God worshiped by other religions"?

5. In view of all you know about the name of Jesus, God's Messiah, what kind of person do you think is being described in 2 John 1:7?

Can you think of some examples in today's culture?

DID YOU KNOW?

The most common compound name of Jesus—"the Lord Jesus Christ"—was originally used as a very technical description of His identity, and today is an extremely accurate description of who He is.

The word for *Lord* in Greek meant "master" or "ruler," which Jesus not only will ultimately be in the future, but should be in each of our lives today. The word *Jesus* is, of course, His human name, which constantly reminds us that He came in human flesh, and was given a name which means "YHWH saves."

Finally, the word we so frequently use, *Christ,* actually was the Greek word for "Messiah," and was used first and foremost by the Jews of that Greek-speaking day. This title alone should be a continual reminder to us that our deepest understanding of who Jesus really is will develop best as we pursue an understanding of God's Messiah, as revealed from the earliest pages of the Old Testament all the way through the final words of Revelation.

🖐 *Celebrate His Love*

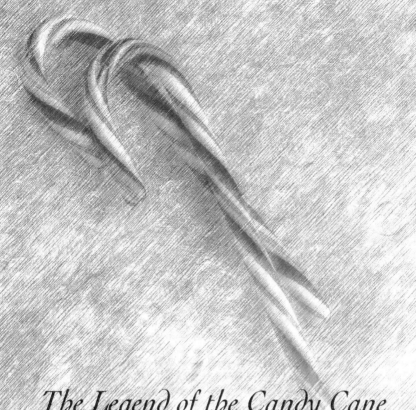

The Legend of the Candy Cane

In the late 18th century in England, all religious symbols were banned from public display. It is said that a dedicated Christian candy maker wanted to provide a way for Christians to identify each other in spite of the restrictions. He began with a piece of white candy to signify the purity of Jesus Christ. Next, he formed the candy into the shape of a shep-herd's staff as a reminder that Jesus is the Good Shepherd. Three small red stripes around the candy represented the power of the Trinity: the Father, the Son, and the Holy Spirit. One bold red stripe through the candy represented the redeeming power of the blood that Christ shed for each of us, and for the forgiveness of our sins.

Loving Jesus at Christmas

This lesson examines the practical issue of loving Christ during the holiday season—and year around—in the same way that Jesus loved the Father.

OUTLINE

There is a way for us to fulfill the longing in our hearts for true intimacy with our Creator. It is seldom discussed, almost never mentioned at this time of the year, but here is the key: The key to loving Jesus is to understand how Jesus loved His Father.

   I. Jesus Loved the Father by Doing What the Father Asked Him to Do

   II. I Love Jesus by Doing What Jesus Asks Me to Do

   III. If I Will Love Jesus as He loved His Father, Jesus Will Do for Me What the Father Did for Him

Christmas is a wonderful time of the year to love Jesus, for all around us are reminders of His birth and His loving death on our behalf. The cradle or the manger reminds us that He came. The tree is a subtle reminder of where He ended up on our behalf, hanging between heaven and earth. The darkness tells us what we were like before Christ came, and all of the lights which illuminate our hearts remind us that Jesus came as the light of the world to bring joy into each of our lives.

I have been asking myself, "If Jesus were physically here today, what would I say to Him, and how different would it be from what I said to Him in my prayer this morning?" If He were to walk in here among us, and move in and out of our homes, and we had an opportunity to express our love to Him at Christmas time, what would we say? How in the world do we, as modern believers, love Jesus at Christmastime? Do we sing Him songs? Do we go to church? Do we care for the poor? Do we give to the church which is His body? All of these are fine, and they may in some measure fulfill the urge we have within us to love Jesus at Christmas, but there is a way that we can love Jesus—not only at Christmas time but throughout the year—that is so evident that we wonder how we could have missed it. It promises to fulfill the longings we have in our hearts, so when the season is over, we don't sit there at 7:00 o'clock on Christmas Day with the bitter aftertaste in our mouth thinking, "Is this all there is? I thought there would be more, and now it is over."

The key to loving Jesus is to understand how Jesus loved His Father.

We can understand how Jesus loved his Father by turning to a passage of Scripture in the Book of Hebrews. Actually, this passage in the Book of Hebrews is an Old Testament passage used in the New Testament by the writer of Hebrews to make a very important point. The point is how Jesus loved his Father at the Incarnation, at Christmastime. How did he do it?

In Hebrews 10:5 we read, "Therefore, when He came into the world, He said: 'Sacrifice and offering You did not desire, but a body You have prepared for Me. In burnt offerings and sacrifices for sin You had no pleasure.' Then I said, 'Behold, I have come—in the volume of the book it is written of Me, to do Your will, O God.'" This is obviously a quotation from Psalm 40, originally spoken by David. But it is a Messianic psalm, a prophetic psalm which speaks into the future the words of the Lord Jesus as He came into the world to be our Savior. Listen to these words from our Lord's lips. He says, "Lo, I come, in the volume of the book it is written of me, to do your will, O God." How did Jesus love his Father?

JESUS LOVED THE FATHER BY DOING WHAT THE FATHER ASKED HIM TO DO

I can't imagine what that day must have been like. It is an eternal day, and I can't even think in terms of eternity. I have said goodbye to my children for short periods of time, some for weeks at a time, some for just days at a time, but can you imagine the Father in heaven saying goodbye to His Son for thirty-some years? He was in fellowship with the Father, but He was sent from heaven into the world to walk among us. That is what He is talking about when He says, "Lo, I come, in the volume of the book it is written, to do your will, O God." Jesus came in total obedience to His father. "I come to do it your way, O God," says one of the translators.

What did that mean to Him in His earthly life? In John 4:34 Jesus continued to reiterate that He was loving His Father by doing the will of His Father: "Jesus said to them, 'My food is to do the will of Him who sent Me, and to finish His work.'"

Notice, too, John 5:30: "I can of Myself do nothing. As I hear I judge; and My judgment is righteous, because I do not seek My own will, but the will of the Father who sent Me."

And in John 6:38: "For I have come down from heaven, not to do My own will, but to do the will of Him who sent Me."

Throughout His life, Jesus was loving His Father. How? Every time He was questioned, Jesus said, "I have not come to do My own will. I have come to do the will of the Father who sent Me."

And then, when it came to that moment of crisis in the Garden of Gethsemane, and the fact that Jesus ultimately would pay the penalty for the sin of the whole world, He came back to this principle again: "Nevertheless, not My will, but Your will be done." How did Jesus love the Father? He loved the Father by doing the will of the Father.

I have written in the front of my Bible a verse. It is just a part of a verse, but it summarizes the life of Jesus while He was on this earth. It is John 8:29: "I always do those things that please [the Father.]"

Every minute Jesus was on the earth, everything He did, every thought He had, was conditioned out of one truth: I want to please My Father.

Was God the Father pleased with Him? On two occasions at least, His pleasure broke out. When Jesus was being baptized the Father said, "This is my beloved Son in whom I am well pleased."

And it happened in Matthew 17, on the Mount of Transfiguration. Jesus was being transfigured. He was being revealed. And the Father said, "This is my beloved Son in whom I am well pleased." Not these other two (Moses and Elijah). This one.

Jesus lived all of His life that He might please the Father. And when the report card came in, the Father said, "This is my beloved Son, in whom I am well pleased" (v.17:5).

I Love Jesus By Doing What Jesus Asks Me to Do

At the beginning we said that if we could understand how Jesus loved His Father, then maybe, just maybe, we can understand how we can love Jesus.

In John 14:21 the Lord Jesus says, "He who has My commandments and keeps them, it is he who loves Me, And he who loves Me will be loved by My Father, and I will love him, and manifest Myself to him."

Notice the first part of the verse: "He who has My commandments and keeps them, it is he who loves me." Always doing that which is pleasing the Father. Remember—if we learn how Jesus loved the Father, we can learn how we can love Jesus.

Then notice verse 23: "Jesus answered and said to him, 'If anyone loves Me, he will keep My word.'" The negative of this is in verse 24: "He who does not love Me does not keep My words." Do you want to know how not to love Jesus at Christmastime? The Scriptures say the way not to love Jesus at Christmastime is not to keep His words.

Finally, look at John 15:10: "If you keep My commandments, you will abide in My love." So let's back up and ask ourselves that question again. How do we love Jesus at Christmastime? Well, how did Jesus love the Father? "In the volume of the Book it is written of me, 'I come to do Your will, O God.'" He was obedient, according to the Book of Philippians, even to the point of death.

IF I WILL LOVE JESUS AS HE LOVED HIS FATHER, JESUS WILL DO FOR ME WHAT THE FATHER DID FOR HIM

Here is the other part of the equation. If we will love Jesus as Jesus loved the Father, Jesus will do for us what the Father did for Him. Look at the second part of John 14:21. Verse 21 says if we will keep His commandments, we will be loved by the Father and Christ will love us and manifest Himself to us. That's the promise He gives us. He says that if we will love the Lord Jesus by obeying His words, then in a very special way we will be loved by the Father, and we will be loved by the Lord Jesus Christ, and the Lord Jesus will reveal himself to us.

Someone might say, "Am I not loved by the Father?" Yes! Are you not loved by Jesus? Yes, if you are a Christian. Does He not reveal Himself to you? Yes He does, in the Scripture. But there's a special kind of manifest presence that comes upon the person whose only joy in life, whose only passion in life, is the passion that Jesus had. That was to do the will of God.

Notice verse 23: "And My Father will love him, and We will come to him and make Our home with him."

Again, look at (John 15:10): "Abide in My love, just as I have kept my Father's commandments and abide in His love." As we look at these verses, we cannot help but see the principle: If I will love Jesus as Jesus loved the Father, then Jesus will do for me what the Father did for His Son.

That means a day is coming which is foretold in the parable of the talents, when you will be able to stand before Him, having served as a faithful servant, and He will say you are a blessed, faithful servant, and invite you to enter into the joy of your Lord.

So, at Christmastime, when we are running around, buying gifts, and trying to stay out of trouble with all of the relatives and all of the in-laws and all of the rest of everything that happens, how do we get through all of this and focus so that we can love Jesus? Here it is.

We love Jesus by doing what He asks us to do: by keeping His commandments. That's the way to have a very merry, and Christ-centered, Christmas.

1. What do the following verses teach us about the Son's obedience to the Father?

   a. Romans 5:19

   b. Philippians 2:6-8

   c. Hebrews 5:8

2. What will be the ultimate outcome of the Son's obedience to the Father?

   a. Psalm 110:1-2

   b. Daniel 7:13-14

   c. Philippians 2:9-11

3. What do you think was the Son's ultimate act of obedience to the Father? (See Matthew 26:39.)

4. What is faith in Christ called in the verses below?

a. 2 Corinthians 9:13

b. 2 Thessalonians 1:7-8

c. 1 Peter 4:7

5. What, then, should be our understanding of the connection between love for Christ and obedience to Christ?

6. How is that reflected in these passages?

a. John 14:15

b. John 14:21-24

 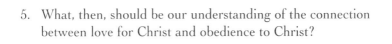 *Celebrate His Love*

c. John 15:10

d. 1 John 2:5-6

7. What does God's Word say about the person who talks about loving Christ, but lives a life of perpetual disobedience (see 1 John 2:4)?

8. In what practical ways, then, might you display your love for Christ during the holiday season and beyond?

DID YOU KNOW?

The history of the Christian church is a continuous record of swinging between the extremes of legalism on one hand and license on the other. The argument against legalism, of course, is that good works can save no one; while the argument against license is that Christ is not unrighteous; therefore His saints should not engage in unrighteous acts.

The Bible teaches neither legalism nor license for the believer. What the Bible teaches is liberty—freedom—from bondage to belief in works that can save one's self, and freedom from a body that cannot produce good works under the duress of the law. Jesus indeed came that He might set us free from the law, so that rather than vowing to do good (which we cannot do) in order to save ourselves (which we likewise cannot do), by faith we can be saved by Him and be set free to live our lives in submission to Him in us, Who can produce good works.

ICE Candles

This activity needs close adult supervision.

You will need the following items:
- clean, empty cardboard milk cartons
- taper candles
- ice, crushed or cubed
- old broken crayons or candles
- candle wax (paraffin)
- old coffee cans

Remove tops from milk cartons and cut to desired height. Center a taper candle in each milk carton, making sure the wick is above the top of the carton. Place carton in a shallow foil-lined pan.

Melt wax in a coffee can that has been placed in a pan of water. Stir wax to aid in melting, and heat to a simmer.

Fill area around taper in carton with ice. The larger the ice cubes and the more ice you use, the larger the holes in the candles. Now is the time to add bits of broken crayons or candles for extra color and texture.

✳ ✳ ✳
The next step should be done by an adult.
✳ ✳ ✳

Pour melted wax over ice in carton slowly. As the wax cools around the ice, it forms holes. Allow to cool completely and pour off water. To remove from carton, simply tear paper gently away from candle.

Just an Ordinary Baby

*This lesson emphasizes the humanity of Jesus
so that we might fully appreciate what
God did when His deity invaded our humanity.*

OUTLINE

The older we get, the more we understand that the real meaning of the holiday is not the giving of gifts (as exciting as that is), but the relationship we have with one another, and the privilege that the holiday provides for us to get together.

But as we enjoy the warmth and joy of our relationships with one another, if we think of it very deeply, we finally contemplate the truth that God so desired a relationship with us that He paid the incredibly supreme price to come and be one of us, so that we might know Him.

   I. At His Birth

  II. During His Childhood

 III. In His Adulthood

In 1 Timothy 3:16 we read, "And without controversy great is the mystery of godliness: God was manifested in the flesh." It is almost as if Paul were overcome by the thought of it.

AT HIS BIRTH

The Apostle Paul bursts out in this epistle with the astonishing words: "Without controversy." In other words, there won't ever be any argument about this. No one can bring an argument against this. "Without controversy, great is the mystery of godliness."

Then he describes the mystery: "God was manifested in the flesh." The only reason we don't say that to one another more often is because we haven't taken the time to comprehend the incredible truth that is involved in God becoming flesh.

In my reading, I have discovered that many of the great writers whom we admire have had moments like Paul had when he wrote 1 Timothy, moments when in the ordinary course of their writing it suddenly dawned on them, it suddenly hit them, it suddenly became part of their frontal lobe thinking, this truth that God has become a man.

A. W. Tozer wrote, "The coming of Jesus Christ into this world represents a truth more profound than any philosophy that the world has ever known. All of the great thinkers of the world together could never have produced anything even remotely approaching the wonder and profundity disclosed in the message of these words: He came. The words are wiser than all learning, and understood in their high spiritual context, they are more eloquent than all oratory, more lyric and moving than all music. They tell us that all of mankind, sitting in darkness, has been visited by the Light of the world."

John the Apostle, writing in the New Testament, said it this way: "The Word became flesh and dwelt among us, and we beheld His glory, the glory as of the only begotten of the Father, full of grace and truth" (John 1:14).

And writing in a more formal way to the Galatians, Paul the Apostle said it in these words: "But when the fullness of the time had come, God sent forth His Son, born of a woman" (Galatians 4:4).

Isaiah the Prophet said it would be like this. In the seventh chapter of his prophecy (Isaiah 7:14), which is quoted by Matthew in the narrative of the birth of Jesus, Isaiah said that His name would be called Immanuel, which, being translated, is "God with us." God coming down to be one of us.

As we've asked ourselves before, is this the way we would have done it? Would this have been your master plan to rescue lost mankind? Would you have had your Redeemer delivered to a manger and wrapped in strips of swaddling cloth? Would you have had Him born in a stable built for cattle? Would you have had His first visitors the hated shepherds of the hillside? Have you ever heard of a royal story quite like that? Paul was right—great is the mystery of godliness! God was manifested in the flesh.

During His Childhood

I would be afraid of God were it not for the fact that He has come to show me that I don't need to be. He has come as a man, to walk among men and reveal Himself to us, one hundred percent God and one hundred percent man, but truly human. And that's what we often forget. It is a mystery, this birth of our Savior, born in Bethlehem so many years ago. Isaiah the Prophet said, Jesus grew up "as a tender plant, and as a root out of dry ground," and, "He has no form or comeliness; and when we see Him there is no beauty that we should desire Him. He is despised and rejected of men, a Man of sorrows and acquainted with grief" (Isaiah 53:2-3).

One writer has interpreted Isaiah's words like this: "There was no splendor or appearance that we should be drawn to Him. He was just an ordinary baby."

It's true that if you and I had lived during the days of our Lord's childhood, and if we had met Him on the street, we would not have nudged each other and said, "Why, there is the young Messiah!" We would not have known. It was not even known by those with whom He grew up.

Even his own brothers did not know that He was the Messiah. He was just an ordinary baby like you and like me. There was nothing that would have set Him apart from us, except the fact that if we were near Him and could have watched His life, you would have understood that He did not sin.

One thing that has captured my attention is that from the day Jesus was born until He was 12 years old, we have no record of Him speaking. Then, when Jesus was 12 years old, He lingered in Jerusalem at the temple after His parents had left to return to Nazareth. When they found Him and asked Him why this had happened, He spoke 17 words in the Jewish language to the effect that, "Did you not know that I must be about My Father's business?"

In His Adulthood

Then in the New Testament we are given the record of His baptism at the age of 30. So all through His life, from the time He was born—with the exception of that time when He was 12—until He was 30 years of age, we have no word from Messiah. No word. Jesus lived His life in those early years in total obscurity. We have no word from His lips for three decades. And then we have His magnificent ministry that was lived out in just three years.

Jesus spent His whole life as we would know it experiencing humanity, living among the common people, going to work every day in his father Joseph's carpenter shop, working alongside his brothers, learning to experience what it is like to be a human being. Not a human being with a halo, because that's not normal human experience, but human life as our lives are.

In Luke 2, just as Luke is concluding this early period of the Lord's life, he provides us with the only sketch of what was going on with Jesus during that time. In Luke 2:40 Luke says of Jesus in His early days, "[He] grew and became strong in spirit, filled with wisdom; and the grace of God was upon Him."

Then, in Luke 2:52 he writes, "and Jesus increased in wisdom and stature, and in favor with God and man." That's it. That's all we have.

All kinds of legends have been invented about His childhood, but they don't come from the Scriptures. The Scriptures are incredibly silent about those years.

This tells me that it was done on purpose, so that God could get through to us that Jesus Christ grew up as one among us—with little being said, little being written, but much being experienced in His life.

There are some things we can arrive at by conjecture. Secular historians tell us that Jesus' father died when He was a very young boy. That is pretty well accepted. If so, then Jesus no doubt would have had to take more responsibility as the older brother in the family and in the family business. It would also mean that He knew what it

Celebrate His Love

meant to lose a parent. He experienced that. It would also mean that He grew up in a single parent home. He knew what that is like as well.

Think for a moment just what those days must have been like. Later, when He was rejected by His brothers, that must have hurt. He knew in His heart that one day He would close the door on that home and walk out into a life that would be chronicled for the rest of history to read about. But how could He say that to James so that it would come through? In fact, in the beginning James didn't believe any of it.

As He got out into His ministry, we know that Jesus felt the pain of being betrayed by a very close friend. Three times, one of His closest friends said that he didn't even know Him. He probably was slandered and lied about more than any human being who ever walked on this earth. Why did that all happen? Because He came to be one of us. He came to walk among us. He came to experience what we experience. Whatever your troubles or trials, Jesus understands all of it, because He has experienced it.

The Bible tells us He was tired, He was thirsty, He wept. Two places in the New Testament say that He was troubled in spirit. Have you ever been troubled in spirit? Jesus understands what that is like. He was hungry, He was often tired, and yes, He was even tempted.

All of that is to say that the ratio of 30 years of living and three years of ministry is so that when He spoke in those three years, He would speak with authority, He would speak as one who could be trusted, and He would speak as one who had lived life as we do. So when He says, "Don't do that," it is not because He is trying to keep us from enjoying a good time. As the Son of God He walked in the soot and dirt and sin and filth of the world, and He saw the pain and anguish of those who violated the holy law.

Hebrews 4:14 tells us, "Seeing then that we have a great High Priest who has passed through the heavens, Jesus the Son of God, let us hold fast our confession. For we do not have a High Priest who cannot sympathize with our weaknesses, but was in all points tempted as we are, yet without sin. Let us therefore come boldly to the throne of grace, that we may obtain mercy and find grace to help in time of need."

We are to come boldly to Jesus Christ not just because He is God, but we can come boldly to Him because He is a friend who understands. He has been there before. He has walked through the thing you are walking through. Whatever pain you have felt, He has felt. In fact, one of the translations of the words "to speak boldly" is "to have free utterance." Come before the Lord with free utterance.

Do you pray like that? Sometimes when I hear Christians praying, and especially when I know how badly they are hurting, I want to put my arm around them and say, "Would you just please tell the Lord what you feel?" He will understand. He is not someone who is removed from us as if a planet in a distant galaxy. He is the Lord who came down. He is the One who became one of us and walked among us and felt every emotion we feel. If you are hurting, He has hurt as you do. Therefore, what a friend He can be to you!

When you pray, you don't have to couch all your prayers in the "thees and thous" of the King James Bible. You can come and tell Him what is in your heart.

Do you know Him like that? Have you cultivated a relationship with Jesus Christ that helps you to have free utterance when you pray?

That's why Christmas is so special. It brings God down, not in a defamatory way, not in a defeating way, but to be one of us so that we can relate to Him. And just as human relationships at Christmas are special, so the relationship we have with Jesus Christ is special because of who He is, how He lived, and what He did.

1. Why do you think it was essential that the Son of God be incarnated as a Baby in Bethlehem?

   Upon what portions of the Bible do you base your thoughts?

2. What stereotypes of Christmas (Christmas scenes, cards, nativity scenes) might we need to rethink if we understand that Jesus was, physically, just an "ordinary baby"?

3. What do you think Paul meant in Philippians 2:7 when he referred to Jesus "coming in the likeness of men"?

What point is he making?

Why do you think that "likeness" is important?

4. What physical trials can you think of that Jesus either endured according to the biblical record, or might have endured because of when and where He lived?

What mistreatment from other people?

Celebrate His Love

5. In Matthew 26:48-49, why do you think Judas needed to provide Jesus' captors with an indication of which Person He was?

How does this compare with the perception that Jesus always stood out in a crowd?

6. What comfort do you personally find in the fact that Jesus was a "common man"?

7. What do the following verses tell us of the benefits of Jesus' coming in the likeness of man?

a. Hebrews 4:15-16

b. Hebrews 12:1-2

c. Hebrews 12:3-4

DID YOU KNOW?

Myths of Jesus performing miraculous or magical feats during His childhood are rampant, especially in the various Eastern religions. And often, Christians do not know how to answer such claims from outside the Bible.

It is essential to remember that through God's covenant with Abraham (Genesis 12, 15, 17), the Messiah was—by God's unconditional contract—promised to Israel first (Romans 1:16), and then to the world through Israel. That is precisely why Jesus went first to the Jews, then after being rejected by the religious leaders, to the population of Israel at large, and to the Gentiles.

Because of that, it was essential that Jesus present Himself first to Israel, through the "signs" Israel required (John 2:18; 1 Corinthians 1:22). These signs were not simply magic tricks; they were local, immediate manifestations of acts that the Old Testament had already revealed only Messiah could do. And—very clearly stated in John 2:11—the very first of these was His miracle of turning purification water into "best wine" at the wedding in Cana of Galilee. That means none—exactly zero—miracles were done by Him as a child.

🖐 *Celebrate His Love*

Donna Jeremiah's Package Code

Four curious children can create a challenge for any mom at Christmastime, so I decided to avoid the constant struggle to hide presents and keep track of which child was shaking, smelling, or unsealing a package to determine what was inside.

I wanted to wrap the packages and put them under our tree in advance of Christmas morning, but keeping an ever-present watch over the activities around the tree was more than this mom could easily handle.

I decided to create a numbering system that would allow me to wrap the packages and affix a name tag, but instead of the name I would code each gift with a multiple digit number. I had to rotate the numbers; our children are clever and could soon figure out who had what number.

On Christmas morning we would distribute the gifts and the children would not have time to guess the contents. My system has proven effective and we still use it.

If God Has Not Forgotten Us, Why Have We Forgotten Him?"

In this lesson we hypothesize what the world would be like if there had been no first Christmas.

OUTLINE

It is hard to comprehend a world without Christ. That is because most of us have grown up in a Christian environment. But perhaps one of the best ways we could comprehend it is to look for just a moment to a period of time after Christ had gone to the cross, then to the grave, then out of the grave in resurrection. And Paul, trying to explain the importance of that to those who would read his letter to the Corinthians, posed a similar question in 1 Corinthians 15. He said in effect, "Let me tell you what life would be like if Christ had not come, if He had not died, if He had not been resurrected from the grave."

    I. A World Without Christ?

   II. A Life Without Christ?

  III. Christmas Without Christ?

A WORLD WITHOUT CHRIST?

In 1 Corinthians 15:14 Paul tells us that if Christ had not come, our preaching would be useless.

In that same verse, he says that if Christ had not come, our faith would be empty.

In verse 15 he said that if Christ had not come, those of us who are Christians would be false witnesses. We would be telling lies because we would be saying something was true when indeed it was not.

In 15:17 he said that if Christ had not come, our faith would be futile, worthless.

He said if Christ had not come we would all still be in our sins. We would be unforgiven.

In verse 18 of that text, he said if Christ had not come, we would never see our dead loved ones again, for those who have died have perished. And then in verse 19 he summarizes it by saying if Christ had not come, we would be the most miserable of all people.

Sometimes the only way we can appreciate what we have as Christians is to realize that everything that's good, and everything that's wholesome, and everything that's positive, and everything that's clean, and everything that's true, has its roots in the Person of the Lord Jesus Christ, who came as the gift of God the Father to be our Savior. It is a wonderful thought to remember that God has not forgotten us.

A LIFE WITHOUT CHRIST?

But the question, then, must be: If God has not forgotten us, then why do we seem to have forgotten Him?

Every Christmas is the coming together of a magnificent occasion and a wonderful opportunity. It is not different from that first Christmas Day recorded for us in Luke 2:1-7:

> And it came to pass in those days that a decree went out from Caesar Augustus that all the world should be registered. This census first took place while Quirinius was governing Syria. So all went to be

registered, everyone to his own city. Joseph also went up from Galilee out of the city of Nazareth, into Judea, to the city of David, which is called Bethlehem, because he was of the house and lineage of David, to be registered with Mary, his betrothed wife, who was with child. So it was that while they were there, the days were completed for her to be delivered. And she brought forth her firstborn Son, and wrapped Him in swaddling cloths, and laid Him in a manger, because there was no room for them in the inn.

I like to think of that night in terms of the kind of silence that is observed in the eastern U.S. when snow falls on Christmas Day, and everything is absolutely still.

On this magnificent night recorded by Luke, we are told that Mary brought forth her firstborn son and wrapped Him in swaddling cloths and laid Him in a manger. It was a magnificent occasion that escaped observation by almost everyone who was there.

We read in John 1 that "The Word was with God, and the Word was God. . . . and the Word became flesh and dwelt among us." At that moment in that silent night when Mary birthed her baby, Deity invaded humanity. In that moment, when Mary birthed her baby, eternity invaded time. And no one really understood that.

Micah the prophet said it this way in his prophecy of Micah 5:2: "But you, Bethlehem Ephrathah, though you are little among the thousands of Judah, yet out of you shall come forth to Me the One to be ruler in Israel, Whose goings forth have been from of old, from everlasting."

How could one be born whose goings forth have been from old, from everlasting? In that moment of time when Mary birthed her baby, Royalty invaded poverty. The One who had all wealth at His disposal, who was the King of glory, who created the world that we love and live in, that same One was birthed to Mary.

What a magnificent occasion! A silent night interrupted by a tiny cry in Bethlehem. This magnificent occasion was set up from eternity past. And it wonderfully met every criterion that was laid out for it.

But, on this night of all nights, it happened in a place where no one even recognized what was going on. The God who had refused to forget us, was forgotten by those to whom He first came. The Bible tells us "He came to His own, and His own did not receive Him" (John 1:11). The King of glory had come down, and He was not recognized or received.

The innkeeper should not have missed it because he was so close to it. Isn't it interesting how we can go through life, and often be so close to the magnificent, and never let it dawn upon our conscious awareness? He was so close. The mother of our Lord was at his door. She was seeking a place to birth the Son of God, and he would not let her in because there was no room.

CHRISTMAS WITHOUT CHRIST?

Am I pressing the point too much when I say that today the world is filled with innkeepers who miss the meaning of Christmas?

If that is not the case, why, as we go through the shopping centers during this season, are there so many grim faces in our stores, so many exhausted, sleepy people in our churches the Sunday before Christmas? The innkeeper missed Christmas not because he was angry or because he was belligerent. He missed Christmas because of ignorant preoccupation. He got so busy with everything that was going on in his life, taking care of the inn, taking care of the census, taking care of all of the pressure, he couldn't stop to reflect upon the moment that was at hand.

Many people today are like that. The chambers of their souls are filled with needless things, stuff that doesn't really matter. They miss the Messiah of God. Oh, how hard it is for us to clear out the chambers of our heart and mind, and make room for the Messiah!

One of the great tragedies of our time is not that God has forgotten us, but that we have forgotten Him. On the same day that Alexander Solzhenitsyn, the Russian-born Nobel prize winner, was presented with the Templeton Foundation Prize for Progress in Religion by Prince Philip at Buckingham Palace, he addressed many of Britain's leading political and religious leaders, including the Archbishop of Canterbury. "Over half a century ago," stated Solzhenitsyn, "while I was still a child, I remember hearing a number of older people offer the following explanation of the great disasters that have befallen Russia. Men have forgotten God. That's why it has all happened. And if I were called upon to identify the principal trait of the entire twentieth century, I would be unable to find anything more precise and more worthy than to repeat, men have forgotten God."

In our world today, doesn't it seem to you that men have forgotten God? And we who have been given this holiday occasion to embrace the Christ because God has not forgotten us, we must ask ourselves in our hearts, "Have I forgotten God?" That is not a question just for those who do not know God through Christ. That is a question for all of us. It is possible for us to live as practical atheists and still be Christians in the sense that we go through our lives without giving any time whatsoever to the One who came to make life meaningful for us. Let us not, at this time of the year, forget the One who has not forgotten us.

Some have heard the gospel message throughout life from a mother's teaching, in Sunday school, or growing up in church. Periodically, you have been reminded that it was for you that this Christ came. But like the innkeeper, you are so busy with everything else you keep pushing Him away. But there is a day coming when He will knock no more. If He knocks at your heart today, you must not forget Him. That is the message of Christmas. You must not forget the One who refused to forget you. Receive Him as your Savior.

APPLICATION

1. If you know Christ today, make a list of as many good things as possible that would not exist in your life if not for your relationship with Him.

2. Which of those events or circumstances were bad things that the Lord Jesus Christ transformed into something good?

3. What, then, is the connection between Christ's resurrection from the dead and His ability to redeem our lives into something good? (See Romans 8:11, 28-31.)

Celebrate His Love

4. In 1 Corinthians 15:12-22, what eventual circumstance is Paul connecting to Christ's resurrection?

Why is that an essential part of every Christian's perspective on the future?

If the resurrection of Christ is not a historical fact, where does that leave every Christian?

5. What has been the historical pattern of great nations that have denied or left their faith in Christ?

In our culture today, what is replacing a belief in the Jesus of the Bible?

What effect is that producing?

6. Do you believe it is possible for a genuine Christian to "forget God" in a practical, day-to-day sense?

Why or why not?

What would you forecast as some of the symptoms of that problem?

7. What would you propose as good "preventative medicine" for not forgetting God?

What would you propose as good solutions for those Christians who have?

8. In what way(s) might the Christmas holiday season afford an opportunity for us to "remember" Him? To encourage others to do the same?

To make Him known to those who don't know Him?

DID YOU KNOW?

Although the story line for the Christmas classic "It's a Wonderful Life" is purely fanciful and fictitious, it has for decades connected with those who feel forgotten and forsaken during the holidays, even pointing many to the God of the Bible and genuine faith in Christ.

For actor James Stewart, the barroom scene in which he cries out to God was so profoundly moving, the tears were real and the experience entirely unique. When he was asked to do another take for the benefit of facial closeups, he flatly refused, admitting that at that precise moment, he felt something of the desperation and hopelessness of those who have nowhere else to turn but the true God. The film editors worked with the one take they had, closeups were engineered by enlarging one frame at a time, and a truly vicarious moment of a desperate man's plea to God made it to the screen.

Stained Glass

Use the final remains of various colors of crayons. Shave each color and create stacks of shavings by color. Let each child create their design by placing the colors in the pattern they create on a piece of waxed paper. Place another piece of paper on top of the crayon shavings and gently but firmly set a hot iron on the paper. To make sure you have the work sur-face protected, place a large piece of foil under the entire project. I also place a piece of waxed paper over the top before I set the iron down.

After the paper has cooled, gently peel the top sheet of paper off and enjoy the beauty of an original stained glass window. You may be sur-prised at the artistic expression in your family.

The Bible and the New Year

*In this lesson we look to the new year ahead and
consider the tremendous changes we might experience
through a fresh commitment to the Word of God.*

OUTLINE

As we begin to think about the new year ahead, we are reminded
again of what the Bible really does for us as God's people. The Bible
has a unique ministry in all of our lives, and there would be no better
plan for the next 365 days than to make a fresh commitment to read,
study, and apply the Word of God.

I. What the Bible Is for You
- a. It Is a Sword
- b. It Is a Mirror
- c. It Is a Hammer
- d. It Is Water
- e. It Is Seed
- f. It Is Silver
- g. It Is Fire
- h. It Is a Lamp
- i. It Is Bread
- j. It Is Honey
- k. It Is Milk
- l. It Is Gold

II. What the Bible Will Do for You
- a. Produce Spiritual Growth
- b. Provide Cleansing
- c. Prevent You from Sinning
- d. Protect You from Satan
- e. Protect You from Discouragement
- f. Promote Success in Whatever You Do
- g. Prepare You for Powerful Praying
- h. Point the Way to Salvation

WHAT THE BIBLE IS FOR YOU

In order to convey to us what the Bible does in a believer's life, the writers of the Word of God, by inspiration of the Holy Spirit, used a number of beautiful metaphors.

The Word of God Is a Sword
The Word of God is called a sword because of its piercing ability, operating with equal effectiveness upon Sinners, Saints, and Satan!

> For the word of God is living and powerful, and sharper than any two-edged sword, piercing even to the division of soul and spirit, and of joints and marrow, and is a discerner of the thoughts and intents of the heart (Hebrews 4:12).

The Word of God Is a Mirror
The Word is called a mirror because it reflects the mind of God and the true condition of man:

> For if anyone is a hearer of the word and not a doer, he is like a man observing his natural face in a mirror; for he observes himself, goes away, and immediately forgets what kind of man he was. But he who looks into the perfect law of liberty and continues in it, and is not a forgetful hearer but a doer of the work, this one will be blessed in what he does (James 1:23-25).

The Word of God Is a Hammer
How many of us have been "hammered" by the Word of God? It drives home and breaks up the stony hearts that we have. The Scriptures say: "Is not My word like . . . a hammer that breaks the rock in pieces?" (Jeremiah 23:29). The Word of God is referred to as a hammer because of its ability both to tear down and to build up!

The Word of God Is Water
The Word of God is called water because of its cleansing, quenching, and refreshing qualities—"That He might sanctify and

cleanse [the church] with the washing of water by the word" (Ephesians 5:26).

The Word of God Is Seed

The Word of God is called seed because, once properly planted, it brings forth life, growth, and fruit: "Having been born again, not of corruptible seed, but incorruptible, through the word of God which lives and abides forever" (1 Peter 1:23).

The Word of God Is Silver

The Word is like silver because of its desirability, its preciousness, its beauty, and its value: "The words of the LORD are pure words, like silver tried in a furnace of earth, purified seven times" (Psalm 12:6).

The Word of God Is Fire

The Word of God is called fire because of its judging, purifying, and consuming abilities: "But His word was in my heart like a burning fire . . ." (Jeremiah 20:9).

The Word of God Is a Lamp

The Word is called a lamp because it shows us where we are now, it guides us to the next step, and it keeps us from falling: "Your word is a lamp to my feet and a light to my path" (Psalm 119:105).

The Word of God Is Bread

The Word is like bread that gives everlasting satisfaction to all who are hungry: "I am the living bread which came down from heaven. If anyone eats of this bread, he will live forever; and the bread that I shall give is My flesh, which I shall give for the life of the world" (John 6:51).

The Word of God Is Honey

The Word of God is like honey bringing the sweet comfort of God's love to all who taste: "More to be desired are they than gold . . . sweeter also than honey and the honeycomb" (Psalm 19:10).

The Word of God Is Milk

The Word is like milk, nourishing the soul to spiritual growth: "As newborn babes, desire the pure milk of the word, that you may grow thereby" (1 Peter 2:2).

The Word of God Is Gold

The Word of God is like gold because of its desirability, beauty, and value: "Therefore I love Your commandments more than gold, yes, than fine gold!" (Psalm 119:127).

Those are just a few of the pictures of the Bible in the Scripture. There are many more. But all of those metaphors are to help us understand the value and the preciousness and the importance of God's wonderful word in our lives.

WHAT THE BIBLE WILL DO FOR YOU

Today, however, we have lost much of that. We have taken the Bible out of the public life of American culture, and look what has happened to us. Look where we are today because God's Word has been removed from the fabric of our society.

But far more disastrous than that, the Word of God has seemed to drop out of the lives of many of the people who claim to be God's people. Therefore at this time of year it would be good for us to examine a number of reasons why we should read the Word of God.

If we begin to understand how this Book can change our lives, it will continue to change our lives even today. Even this week. The Word of God is a powerful tool, a change agent in the life of anyone who will take it seriously. So I would like to offer my top eight reasons why we should read the Word of God.

It Will Produce Spiritual Growth

Every year at this time, I take a little inventory and ask myself, "Have I grown in the Lord this year? Has there been growth in my life?"

There is absolutely no human way we will ever grow in our faith apart from a personal, disciplined reading and studying of the Word of God. There is no other means of growth. Consider what the Word of God says:

> "As newborn babes, desire the pure milk of the word, that you may grow thereby" (1 Peter 2:2).
> "All Scripture is given by inspiration of God, and is profitable for doctrine, for reproof, for correction, for instruction in righteousness, that the man of God may

be complete, thoroughly equipped for every good work" (2 Timothy 3:16-17).

Look at that verse and see how the Word of God helps you grow. First, the Word of God is profitable for doctrine—it shows you the right way to go.

And then it is profitable for reproof—to convict you when you get off that path.

And then it is profitable for correction—to show you how to get back on the path you left.

And then it is profitable for instruction in righteousness—to show you, in a positive way, how to stay on that path in the future.

That's how we grow. That's a great reason to read the Word of God.

It Will Provide Cleansing for Your Life

How many of us know that we live in a toxic environment? Not just physically toxic, but spiritually toxic. Everywhere we go somebody is trying to put something into our hearts, something into our lives, that's going to begin to erode our spiritual walk with the Lord. How do we cleanse our lives from that? How do we keep our lives from being overwhelmed by the toxicity of the world in which we live?

"That He [Christ] might sanctify and cleanse it [the Church] with the washing of water by the word" (Ephesians 5:26).

Jesus, speaking to His disciples, says, "You are already clean because of the word which I have spoken to you" (John 15:3).

The Word of God cleanses our hearts! If we bring the Word of God in, it pushes out the toxicity that we have gathered through the world, cleansing our hearts and making us clean.

Listen to what David said in Psalm 119:9: "How can a young man cleanse his way? By taking heed according to Your word."

In John 17:17, the Lord Jesus prayed that this would be true in our lives in His high-priestly prayer: "Sanctify them by Your truth. Your word is truth."

It Will Prevent You from Sinning

If you get into the Word of God, you won't sin nearly as much as if you don't. The Word of God will prevent you from sinning. That's what David meant again when he said, "Your word I have hidden in my heart, that I might not sin against You" (Psalm 119:11).

The more you are in the Word of God, the more sensitive you become to those things which can lead you astray. It is awfully difficult to spend an hour or two in the Word of God in the morning, and then walk away from that and begin to violate principles that you know are a part of God's truth. The Word of God empowers you to do the right thing, so you don't end up violating what you know to be true.

> "Direct my steps by Your word, and let no iniquity have dominion over me" (Psalm 119:133).

> "The law of his God is in his heart; none of his steps shall slide" (Psalm 37:31).

The more you get into the Word of God and study it, the more it will help you to stay away from things that will ultimately destroy you.

It Will Protect You from Satan

The Word of God is the greatest protection you have. Of course, someone might say, "I don't believe in Satan."

That, however, doesn't make any difference. He is real anyway. Satan is alive and well, and we are in a daily warfare against the enemy of our souls. Satan goes around as a roaring lion seeking whom he may devour. He wants to take you and drown any influence you have. He wants to ruin you for anything you ever want to do for the Lord.

So how do you protect yourself against Satan? Let's look at the Lord Jesus Christ, who was taken to the desert and was tempted. How did the Lord meet the temptation?

In Matthew 4:4-10, Jesus fought the enemy with the Word of God. If you know God's Word and you are in the Word of God, you put Satan at a disadvantage because you have the power of God's Word working in your life.

Celebrate His Love

It Will Protect You from Discouragement

There were two disciples on one occasion who left Jerusalem after the Crucifixion. They were depressed and discouraged because they thought it was "all over." Christ had died, and they did not know that He was resurrected. They were walking toward Emmaus talking about their hopelessness and they were sad and depressed and discouraged about the situation they saw. Then all of a sudden Jesus came alongside and began to talk with them. And after Jesus had encouraged them, they said, "Did not our heart burn within us while He talked with us on the road, and while He opened the Scriptures to us?" (Luke 24:32).

When you get to the point where you're discouraged and don't know what to do, go to the Friend that sticks closer than a brother, and listen to His Word. If you will discipline yourself to do that, you will discover like these disciples that your heart will begin to burn within you. God's Word will come in, dissipate those discouraging thoughts, take away the things that would drive you down, and begin to lift you up. God's Word has the power to protect you from discouragement.

It Will Promote Success in Whatever You Do

Being in the Word of God gives you the opportunity to be more successful than you would ever be otherwise.

In fact, Psalm 1:1-3 tells us:

> Blessed is the man who walks not in the counsel of
> the ungodly, nor stands in the path of sinners, nor sits
> in the seat of the scornful; but his delight is in the law
> of the LORD, and in His law he meditates day and
> night. He shall be like a tree planted by the rivers of
> water, that brings forth its fruit in its season, whose
> leaf also shall not wither; and whatever he does shall
> prosper.

Whenever you are in the Word of God, you are in a position to be successful in what you do. And if we use the Word of God's definition of success, we can really see how that works. The Word of God promises us that when we make it the substance of our life, it will help us to succeed in what we do.

It Will Prepare You for Powerful Praying

Consider John 15:7: "If you abide in Me, and My words abide in you, you will ask what you desire, and it shall be done for you."

How does that work? It helps you to know what to ask for. When you read the Word of God, you get a sense of God's will, and when you ask in God's will, He gives it to you. So it will prepare you for how you are to pray.

It Will Point the Way to Salvation

That's what this Book is all about. Paul wrote to young Timothy, ". . . as for you, continue in the things which you have learned and been assured of, knowing from whom you have learned them, and that from childhood you have known the Holy Scriptures, which are able to make you wise for salvation through faith which is in Christ Jesus" (2 Timothy 3:14-15).

How does a person become a Christian? Through this Book. The plan of salvation is in this Book. Christ died for you and for your sin, and He paid the penalty that you should have paid, and He died on the cross for you. That message is in this Book.

Are you in the Word? If not, start now reading the Word of God. Find some time in the morning to spend a few moments with God and his Word.

Now, if you are not a Christian, you won't have the motivation to do that. Further, you won't understand a word of it when you read it. If you aren't a Christian, you don't have the ability to comprehend the Word of God as He meant it to be understood. The first step in understanding the Word of God is knowing the God of the Word. And you can't know Him unless you put your trust in Jesus Christ as your personal savior.

You can do that through a simple prayer. Say, "Lord God, I come to You on this first Sunday of the New Year to give my heart to You. I ask You to forgive my sin and cleanse my life, and I accept Your free gift of eternal life which You died to provide for me."

Christ will come into your life if you will let Him, if you will ask Him. As we begin to think about the New Year ahead, we are reminded again of what the Bible really does for us as God's people. The Bible has a unique ministry in all of our lives. And the Bible will come alive for you.

1. If the Bible is everything mentioned in this lesson, why do you think Christians tend to neglect it? Name as many reasons as you can think of.

2. What do the following passages indicate about the connection between God and His Word, or between knowing God and knowing His Word:

   a. John 1:1-2, 14

b. John 17:17

c. 1 John 5:7

d. Revelation 19:13

3. Read Mark 12:30, then read Psalm 119:97; 119:113; 119:163. Why is the Psalmist not guilty of idolatry (for loving the Word)?

4. What is the means of spiritual growth and maturity, according to:

   a. Hebrews 5:12-14

   b. 1 Peter 2:2

5. What do you think Paul is admonishing Timothy to do in
   2 Timothy 2:15? Is this something only for select Christians, or
   for all Christians?

6. Turn to Psalm 119 and, taking no more than five minutes for
   each, find:

   a. As many different names for the Word of God as you can.

   b. As many benefits of the Word of God as you can.

7. Briefly write out, for your eyes only, your personal desires and goals for the coming year, in relation to God's Word and your commitment to it. Tape it inside your Bible where you can find it easily, and read it at least once per week for the coming year.

DID YOU KNOW?

Until publication of the King James Bible in the early 1500s, it was unusual for anyone to possess the Scriptures in the common language. Even then, initial publication was one Bible per official (state-approved) church, kept either under lock and key, or permanently attached to an immovable pulpit. It would be another 200 years or so before individually printed Bibles would begin making their way into the hands and homes of "everyday" Christians—and then largely for the rich alone.

Of course, with the colonization of America, Bibles began making their way to the New World, but only sparsely until printing houses were established and Bibles became an affordable commodity.

That means that the availability of personal Bibles is, in the grand scheme of church history, a fairly recent phenomenon. Even more recent is the phenomenon of multiple personal Bibles—which sit on shelves, collecting dust, and remaining largely unread and unstudied.

It's hard to believe that only 500 years or so in the past, Christians died for proposing the right to personal study of the Scriptures; and today Christians are effectively dead for a lack of it.

May it not be so in the year ahead!

Celebrate His Love

NOTES

NOTES

NOTES

Turning Point
Resource Books
By Dr. David Jeremiah

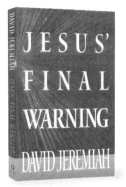

Jesus' Final Warning

Drawing from the Olivet Discourse in the book of Matthew and other Scriptures, Jesus' Final Warning lays out priorities for believers in an era of heightened stress and confusion. Some of Jesus' words comfort, still others rebuke, but not one of His words will ever pass away. In this book, Dr. David Jeremiah offers perspective and timely insights from the Lord Jesus Christ for what may be the best days to proclaim Christ since the first century.
JFWHBK (Hard Cover Book) **$19**
JFWSG (Study Guide) **$9**

Gifts from God

In the pages of *Gifts from God*, Dr. David Jeremiah comes alongside parents to say, "Be encouraged." When it's so easy for parents to be overwhelmed by the responsibilities and challenges of parenting, this book reminds us that we can raise godly children. Through personal and biblical examples, Dr. Jeremiah explains the scriptural model for turning your home into a household of faith. This book will help you realize that children are Gifts from God—straight from His heart to yours.
GFGHBK (Hard Cover Book) **$19**
GFGSG (Study Guide) **$9**

God in You

Many Christians find the Holy Spirit the hardest person of the Holy Trinity to understand. Leaving abstract concepts behind, this book reveals God's Spirit in concrete terms. It brings a fresh, clear image of how the Holy Spirit affects our everyday lives as God is in us and with us.
GIYHBK (Hard Cover Book) **$19**
GIYSG 1, 2 (Study Guide, 2 volumes) **$18**

Prayer—The Great Adventure

Dr. David Jeremiah explores "The Lord's Prayer," which Jesus gave to His disciples, and explains how you can put that pattern into practice in your own life. As you study this prayer and begin to implement our Lord's teaching, you'll become more thankful for what He has done and begin to see His power at work.
PGAHBK (Hard Cover Book) **$19**
PGASG (Study Guide) **$9**

ORDER 1-800-947-1993

Turning Point
Resource Books
By Dr. David Jeremiah

Escape the Coming Night:
The Bright Hope of Revelation
Let Dr. David Jeremiah be your guide through
the terrifying heights and unfathomable depths of the
Book of Revelation. Arm yourself with prophetic truth
about things to come so you can live every moment for
God, because the end is near.
REVBK (Soft Cover Book) $13
REVSG 1, 2, 3, 4 (Study Guide, 4 volumes) $36

The Handwriting on the Wall:
Secrets from the Prophecies of Daniel
Daniel, divinely inspired, accurately prophesied the rise
and fall of empires and their rulers. We cannot pass Daniel off
as just the man in the lion's den or the "dreamer." To know
Daniel is to know how to live today and look
into the future with confidence.
HOWBK (Soft Cover Book) $12
HOWSG 1, 2, 3 (Study Guide, 3 volumes) $27

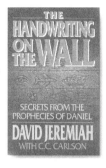

Invasion of Other Gods:
The Seduction of New Age Spirituality
Far too many Christians nowadays are unknowingly dabbling
in occult practices which threaten to shipwreck their faith in
Christ. Many are being caught in subtle satanic traps as they seek
answers to life's pain and problems, or as they search for some
missing spiritual dimension.
    Dr. Jeremiah's warning has become even more urgent.
The "savage wolves" Paul warned of are even now encircling
our homes—but they have learned to speak our language and
they are dressed for success.
IOGBK (Soft Cover Book) $13
IOGSG (Study Guide) $9

What the Bible Says About Angels
Dr. Jeremiah goes straight to God's Word to deliver
fascinating insights about angels, God's majestic messen-
gers. You'll learn that the Bible's rich teaching on angels
is not a trivial fad but a fascinating doorway into sound,
life-giving, spiritual truth that will help you draw closer
than ever to the God you serve.
ANGHBK (Hard Cover Book) $19
ANGSG (Study Guide) $9

ORDER 1-800-947-1993

OTHER STUDY GUIDES & BOOKS AVAILABLE THROUGH TURNING POINT

Audiocassette albums are also available. For information use our toll-free number.

STUDY GUIDES	CODE	QTY	PRICE	TOTAL
20:20 Network Leader's Guide	20:20G	____	$ 9	$ _____
Escape the Coming Night (Revelation, 4 volumes)	REVSG1,2,3,4	____	$ 36	_____
The Power of Encouragement	POESG	____	$ 9	_____
For Such a Time As This—The Book of Esther	ESTSG	____	$ 9	_____
Ten Burning Questions from Psalms	TBQSG	____	$ 9	_____
Knowing the God You Worship	KGWSG	____	$ 9	_____
Seeking Wisdom—Finding Gold	WISSG	____	$ 9	_____
The Handwriting on the Wall (Daniel, 3 volumes)	HOWSG1,2,3	____	$ 27	_____
Invasion of Other Gods (New Age)	IOGSG	____	$ 9	_____
Worship	WORSG	____	$ 9	_____
Turning Toward Integrity (James)	TTIBK	____	$ 10	_____
Turning Toward Joy (Philippians)	TTJSG	____	$ 9	_____
Turning Toward Joy (Philippians)	TTJBK	____	$ 10	_____
The Power of Love (1 Corinthians 13)	POLSG	____	$ 9	_____
Spiritual Warfare (Ephesians 6)	SPWSG	____	$ 9	_____
The Fruit of the Spirit (Galatians 5:16-26)	FOSSG	____	$ 9	_____
Home Improvement	HMISG	____	$ 9	_____
What the Bible Says About Angels	ANGSG	____	$ 9	_____
Greatest Stories Ever Told (Parables)	GSTSG	____	$ 9	_____
A Nation in Crisis (Joshua, 2 volumes)	NICSG1,2	____	$ 18	_____
When Wisdom Turns to Foolishness (Solomon)	WTFSG	____	$ 9	_____
Signs of the Second Coming (Matthew 24 & 25)	SSCSG	____	$ 9	_____
Core Values of the Church (1 Corinthians, 3 volumes)	CVCSG1,2,3	____	$ 27	_____
How to Be Happy According to Jesus (Beatitudes)	HTHSG	____	$ 9	_____
God Meant It for Good (Life of Joseph, 2 volumes)	JOSSG1,2	____	$ 18	_____
Christ's Death and Resurrection	CDRSG	____	$ 9	_____
Prayer—The Great Adventure	PGASG	____	$ 9	_____
The Life of David: The Tender Warrior (2 volumes)	TTWSG1,2	____	$ 18	_____
How to Live According to Jesus (2 volumes)	HTLSG1,2	____	$ 18	_____
The Runaway Prophet—Jonah	TRPSG	____	$ 9	_____
God in You (Holy Spirit, 2 volumes)	GIYSG1, 2	____	$ 18	_____
Ruth, Romance & Redemption	RRRSG	____	$ 9	_____
Gifts from God	GFGSG	____	$ 9	_____
Jesus' Final Warning (Prophecy)	JFWSG	____	$ 9	_____
Celebrate His Love	CHLSG	____	$ 9	_____
BOOKS				
The Handwriting on the Wall (Daniel)	HOWBK	____	$ 12	_____
Escape the Coming Night (Revelation)	REVBK	____	$ 13	_____
The Power of Encouragement	POEBK	____	$ 13	_____
Invasion of Other Gods (New Age)	IOGBK	____	$ 13	_____
What the Bible Says About Angels	ANGHBK	____	$ 19	_____
Prayer—The Great Adventure	PGAHBK	____	$ 19	_____
God in You (The Holy Spirit)	GIYHBK	____	$ 19	_____
Gifts from God (Parenting)	GFGHBK	____	$ 19	_____
Jesus' Final Warning (Prophecy)	JFWHBK	____	$ 19	_____

For information
and Discover, Visa,
or MasterCard
orders, call:

1-800-947-1993

Postage and Handling Chart

For Orders	Add
Up to $5.99	$1.50
$6.00-$19.99	$2.50
$20.00-$50.99	$3.50
$51.00-$99.99	$6.00
$100.00 & over	$9.00

MERCHANDISE TOTAL	_____
SHIPPING/HANDLING	_____
SUBTOTAL	_____
CA RESIDENTS ONLY ADD 7.25% TAX	_____
GIFT TO MINISTRY	_____
TOTAL	$ _____

Please enclose payment with order. Make check or money order payable to:
Turning Point • P.O. Box 3838 • San Diego, CA 92163-1838 *(Please allow 4-6 weeks for delivery.)*

Mr/Mrs/Miss _____

Address _____

City/State/Zip _____

I listen to *Turning Point* on (station call letters): _____ Phone _____